AI in Busi

Boosting Growth and Efficiency

Professor Alamgir Hossain

CEO, Digital Readiness & Intelligent Systems Ltd, UK

Former: Professor & Research Lead of the Centre for Digital Innovation (Teesside University, UK); Professor & Director of IT Research Institute, Anglia Ruskin University (Cambridge, UK); Professor & CIG Research Group Lead, Northumbria University at Newcastle (UK), Vice President CamTech University, Cambodia, Chairman Dept of Computer Sc & Eng., University of Dhaka, Bangladesh.

ISBN: 9798875783456

Table of Content

Preface

AI in Businesses: Boosting Growth and Efficiency is a pivotal resource for anyone interested in harnessing the power of artificial intelligence in the business realm. This book is crafted with the intent to make AI accessible and understandable to a diverse range of readers, including those without extensive technical or mathematical backgrounds. It simplifies complex AI concepts, making them relatable and applicable to everyday business scenarios. Whether you're a seasoned professional, an entrepreneur, or a student curious about AI's role in business innovation, this book is tailored for you. It navigates through the nuances of AI, from fundamental principles to advanced applications, demonstrating how AI can be a game-changer in various industries. The book aims to empower readers to leverage AI technologies effectively to enhance business growth, efficiency, and competitive edge by providing real-world examples and actionable strategies. Join us on this enlightening journey to explore how AI can redefine the future of business.

Abstract

This book is a comprehensive guide that presents artificial intelligence's transformative power in business. It clarifies AI technologies and showcases their potential in enhancing business operations, decision-making, and customer experiences. The book offers practical insights and strategies for integrating AI into various business sectors, emphasising innovation, efficiency, and competitiveness. It targets a diverse audience, making complex AI concepts accessible to non-technical professionals while providing valuable knowledge for those with a technical background. This book is a valuable resource for business leaders, managers, and entrepreneurs seeking to leverage AI for business growth and innovation.

Acknowledgment

I extend my heartfelt gratitude towards the diligent research assistants and colleagues, Mr Hesam Rostamali and Dr Moniruzzaman Bhuiyan, who contributed to this book. Their efforts played a significant role in the creation of this comprehensive resource. Further, I wish to express my appreciation for the language model ChatGPT, whose assistance was instrumental in the preparation of this book. The combined efforts of human intellect and advanced AI have ensured this book will serve as a beneficial guide for a broad spectrum of business, education and other stakeholders.

Chapter 1:

Introduction

1.1 Fundamentals of AI and Systems

What is AI?

Artificial Intelligence (AI) is a field of computer science that aims to create machines that can perform tasks that typically require human intelligence, such as perception, reasoning, learning, and decision-making. AI can be defined as the development and implementation of advanced algorithms that enable machines or systems to perform tasks with a high level of effectiveness, mimicking or surpassing human capabilities in various domains. There are two main approaches to AI: human intelligence and nature-inspired intelligence.

Human intelligence AI is based on the idea that human thinking and reasoning can be modelled and replicated in machines. This approach involves developing algorithms that are based on human cognitive processes, such as perception, attention, memory, and decision-making. Examples of human intelligence AI include expert systems, rule-based systems, and decision trees.

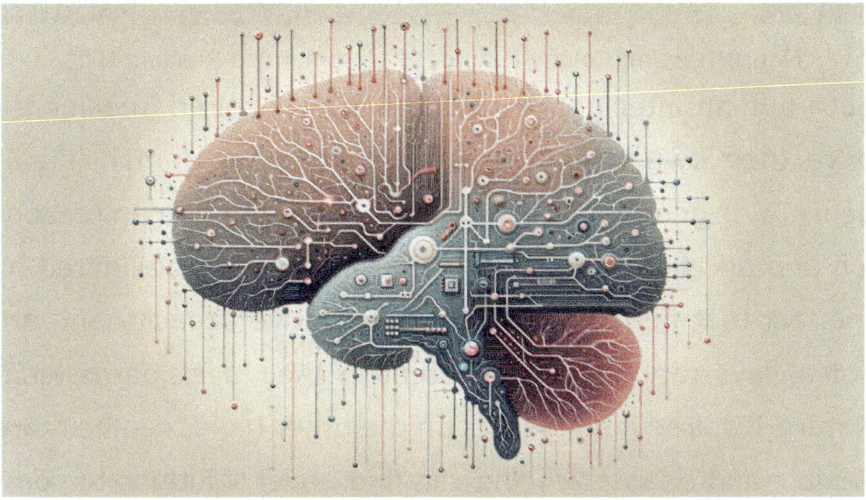

Figure 1.1: Interconnected Neurons of Human Brain (AI Generated)

On the other hand, **nature-inspired intelligence** is based on the idea that biological systems and ecological processes can provide inspiration for the development of intelligent systems. This approach involves developing algorithms that mimic the behaviour and processes of natural systems, such as genetic algorithms, artificial neural networks, and swarm intelligence.

Figure 1.2: Ant Colony (Source: Recommended Reading List)

Both human intelligence AI and nature-inspired intelligence have their own strengths and weaknesses. Human intelligence AI is good at modelling and replicating human reasoning and decision-making processes, but it can be limited by the fact that humans have finite cognitive capacity and are not always rational or consistent in their decision-making. Nature-inspired intelligence, on the other hand, can be more flexible and adaptable, and can find novel solutions to complex problems, but it can be difficult to understand and interpret the reasoning behind its decisions.

Overall, both human intelligence and nature-inspired intelligence have important roles to play in the development of AI systems. By combining the strengths of these approaches, we can create more efficient and adaptive systems that can solve complex problems and improve decision-making in a wide range of applications.

1.2 Growth of AI in Businesses

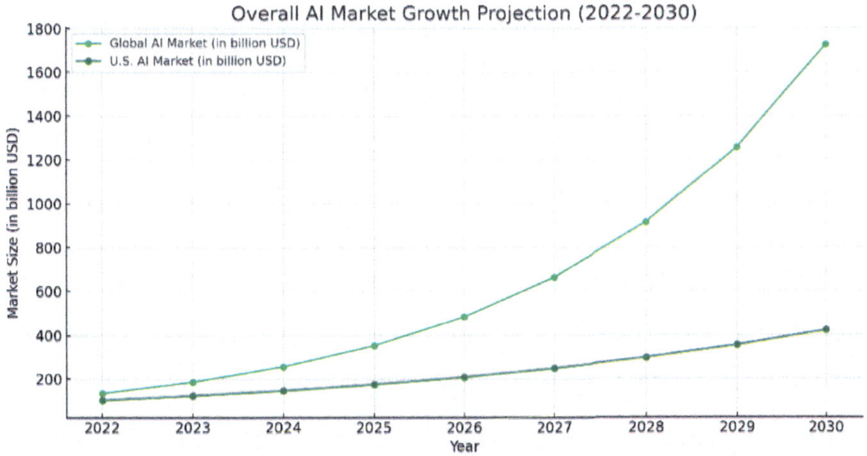

Figure:1.3: AI generated prediction using info from Google Bard

AI is revolutionising the business landscape across various sectors, from customer service to marketing to product development. This section presents the factors driving the growth of AI in businesses, the positive impacts it brings, the challenges it poses, and specific examples of AI implementations in today's business world.

Factors Driving the Growth of AI in Businesses:

Increasing Availability of Data: The proliferation of data in the digital age has provided a rich resource for AI algorithms to learn and improve their performance. As businesses continue to accumulate vast amounts of data from various sources, AI's potential to make informed decisions and predictions also increases (Source: Forbes).

Decreasing Cost of Computing Power: The computational demands of AI algorithms have historically been costly, hindering its widespread adoption. However, the cost of computing power has been steadily decreasing in recent years, making it more affordable for businesses to implement AI solutions (Source: MIT Technology Review).

Growing Expertise in AI: Though AI is a relatively new field, there has been a surge in experts and professionals well-versed in AI technologies. This growing pool of expertise assists businesses in selecting the most suitable AI solutions for their specific needs and effectively implementing them (Source: Harvard Business Review).

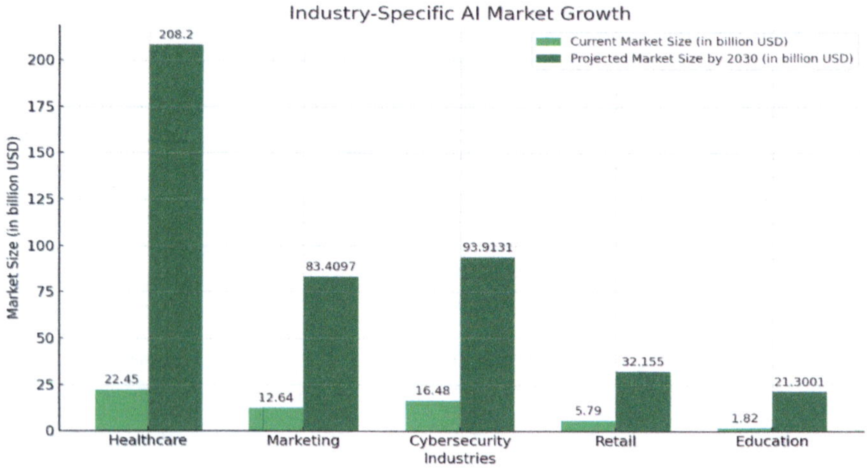

Figure 1.4: AI generated prediction

Positive Impacts of AI in Businesses:

Improved Customer Service: AI applications, such as automated customer support tickets and chatbots, enhance customer service by efficiently handling routine queries. This allows human customer service representatives to focus on more complex issues, resulting in higher customer satisfaction (Source: McKinsey).

Increased Efficiency: AI automation streamlines various tasks, such as data entry and scheduling, which reduces the burden on employees. With ordinary tasks offloaded to AI systems, human resources can dedicate more time to strategic activities, ultimately boosting overall efficiency (Source: Deloitte).

Better Decision-Making: AI's ability to analyse vast datasets and generate valuable insights enables businesses to make more informed decisions across diverse functions, including product development, marketing campaigns, and resource allocation (Source: PwC).

Challenges Associated with AI Implementation in Businesses:

Need for Sufficient Data: To achieve meaningful results, AI algorithms require substantial amounts of quality data. Businesses must ensure they have access to reliable and diverse datasets to harness AI's full potential (Source: VentureBeat).

Requirement for AI Expertise: The complexity of AI systems necessitates businesses to have access to skilled AI professionals who can effectively implement, maintain, and troubleshoot AI solutions (Source: World Economic Forum).

Potential for Bias: AI algorithms can inherit biases from their training data, leading to unfair or inaccurate outcomes. Businesses must be vigilant in identifying and mitigating bias to ensure ethical and unbiased AI applications (Source: Harvard Business Review).

Overall, the rapid growth of AI in businesses has brought about numerous positive transformations, including improved customer service, increased efficiency, and more informed decision-making. However, challenges relating to data availability, expertise, and bias need to be addressed proactively. As AI technology continues to evolve, it is certain to unlock even more innovative and ground-breaking applications across diverse industries (Source: McKinsey Quarterly).

Examples of AI Implementation in Businesses:

Customer Service: Amazon employs AI to address customer queries about their products and services, utilising chatbots and automated customer support systems.

Marketing: Facebook utilizes AI algorithms to target advertisements based on user interests and demographics, optimizing marketing efforts and enhancing return on investment.

Product Development: Netflix leverages AI to analyse user data and preferences, providing personalised movie and TV show recommendations, thus enhancing their content offerings and meeting customer demands more effectively.

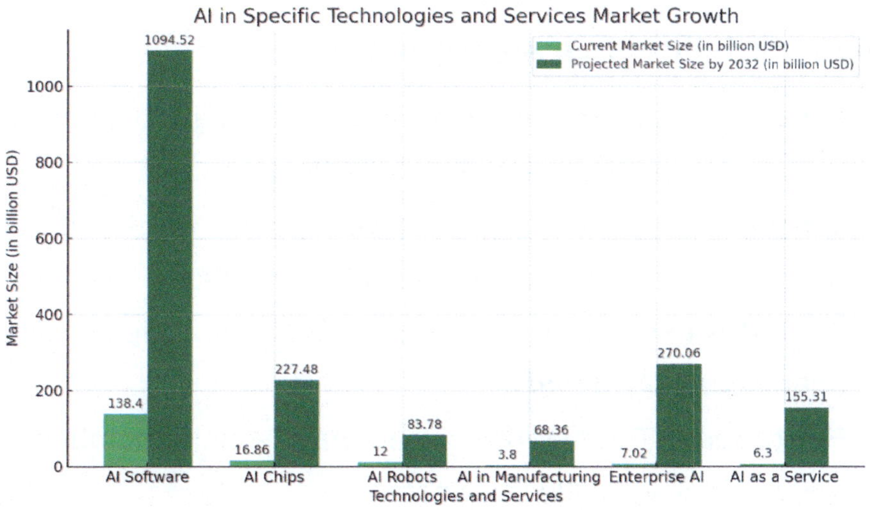

Figure 1.5: Global AI Market (AI Generated)

1.3 Basics of Algorithms and Systems

Algorithms:

An algorithm is a well-defined, step-by-step procedure or set of rules designed to solve a specific problem or perform a particular task. Algorithms are used in many disciplines, including mathematics, computer science, and engineering, to process information, perform calculations, and make decisions.

In computer science, algorithms are the fundamental building blocks for creating computer programs. They are typically written in a programming language and executed on a computer to automate tasks or solve problems efficiently.

Characteristics of an Algorithm:

- **Input**: It takes one or more inputs, which are the values or data required to perform a specific task.
- **Output**: It produces one or more outputs, which are the results or solutions derived from the inputs.
- **Definiteness**: Each step in the algorithm is clearly and unambiguously defined.
- **Finiteness**: The algorithm must have a finite number of steps and eventually terminate.
- **Effectiveness**: Each step in the algorithm must be simple and executable, producing a definite output.

Examples of common algorithms include sorting algorithms (e.g., bubble sort, quicksort), search algorithms (e.g., binary search, linear search), and pathfinding algorithms (e.g., Dijkstra's algorithm, A* search algorithm).

Systems:

A system is a set of interconnected components that function together to achieve a specific goal. Some key concepts in systems include:

- **Components**: The building blocks of a system, such as hardware, software, people, or processes.
- **Relationships**: The connections and interactions between components that determine the system's behaviour.
- **Boundaries**: The limits that define the scope and extent of a system.
- **Feedback**: The process through which a system receives information about its performance and adjusts accordingly.
- **Homeostasis**: The ability of a system to maintain a stable internal environment despite external changes.

Types of Systems:

Systems can be categorised based on various criteria, including their complexity, purpose, and domain. Some common types of systems include:

- **Natural systems**: Systems found in nature, such as ecosystems, the solar system, and human bodies.
- **Artificial systems**: Human-made systems designed for specific purposes, such as transportation, communication, or manufacturing.

- **Open systems**: Systems that exchange matter, energy, or information with their environment, such as living organisms.
- **Closed systems**: Systems that do not exchange matter or energy with their environment, such as isolated chemical reactions.
- **Cybernetic systems**: Systems that use feedback to maintain a desired state, such as thermostats or autopilots.

Information Systems:

Information systems are designed to support the management and use of information in organisations. They typically involve a combination of hardware, software, data, people, and processes to achieve their objectives. Information systems can be classified into various categories, such as:

- **Transaction processing systems (TPS)**: These systems record and process routine transactions, such as sales, purchases, or payroll.
- **Management information systems (MIS)**: These systems provide information to support decision-making at the managerial level.
- **Decision support systems (DSS)**: These systems assist decision-makers in analysing complex problems and exploring alternative solutions.

- **Executive information systems (EIS)**: These systems provide top-level managers with easy access to relevant information and performance indicators.
- **Expert systems (ES)**: These systems use artificial intelligence techniques to mimic human expertise in specific domains.

Applications of Information Systems:

Information systems play a vital role in various sectors and industries, enabling organizations to enhance productivity, improve decision-making, and gain a competitive advantage. Some common applications of information systems include:

- **Enterprise resource planning (ERP)**: Integrating various business functions, such as finance, human resources, and inventory management, to streamline operations and support data-driven decision-making.
- **Customer relationship management (CRM)**: Managing interactions with customers and prospects to improve customer satisfaction, loyalty, and profitability.
- **Supply chain management (SCM)**: Coordinating the flow of goods, information, and resources between suppliers, manufacturers, and customers to optimise efficiency and responsiveness.
- **Knowledge management systems (KMS)**: Capturing, organising, and sharing knowledge within an organisation to foster learning, innovation, and collaboration.

- **E-commerce**: Leveraging digital technologies to conduct business transactions, market products, and engage with customers online.

By harnessing the power of information systems, organisations can improve their decision-making processes, streamline operations, and enhance their competitiveness in an increasingly digital world. As technology continues to evolve, it is crucial for businesses to stay updated with the latest advancements in information systems and adopt them to drive growth and innovation.

Relationship Between Algorithms and Systems: The relationship between an algorithm and a system can be understood as the role that the algorithm plays in the overall functioning and organisation of the system. A system is typically a collection of interrelated components or processes working together to achieve a specific goal or to perform a particular function. In the context of computing or information systems, these components may include hardware, software, data, and people.

Figure: 1.6: Open Loop Multi-inputs and Multi-output System

An algorithm serves as a fundamental building block within a system, providing the logic and rules for processing information, making decisions, or executing specific tasks. It is an essential part of the software component of the system. The system uses algorithms to achieve its goals efficiently and accurately, while the algorithms themselves rely on the system's resources (e.g., memory, processing power, input/output devices) to execute their operations.
In summary, the relationship between an algorithm and a system can be described as follows:

- The algorithm is a key component of the system, providing the logic and rules for specific tasks or problem-solving.
- The system provides the necessary resources, such as hardware and software, for the algorithm to function and execute its operations.
- The performance and efficiency of a system can depend on the algorithms it employs. Well-designed algorithms can lead to more efficient and accurate systems.
- The system's architecture and design can influence the choice and implementation of algorithms. In some cases, the system may need to be adapted or redesigned to accommodate specific algorithms.
- Algorithms and systems are often developed and optimised together to ensure the best possible performance and outcomes.

Figure 1.7: Feedback Systems to Adjust with Target Outputs

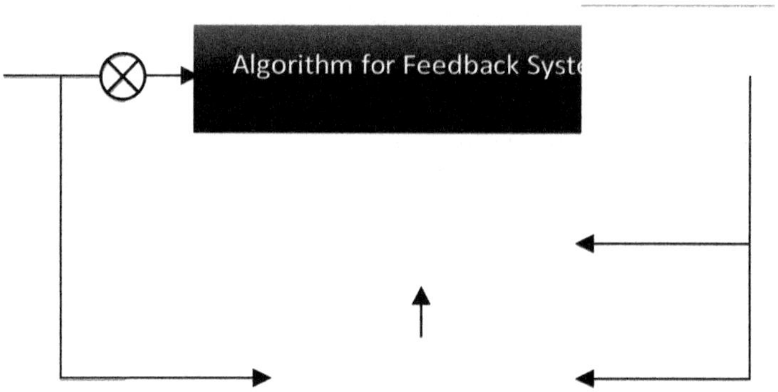

Figure 1.8: Dynamic Adaptive System through Reinforcing Feedback Parameters

Figure 1.6, 1.7 and 1.8 shows three different commonly used systems. Understanding feedback look and reinforcement models are essential terminologies to read this book.

Chapter 2:

AI Algorithms & Applications

2.1 Introduction

AI algorithms are the building blocks of AI systems. They are mathematical models that allow machines to process and analyse data, learn from it, and make predictions or decisions. The most commonly used AI algorithms can be considered under three categories: machine learning, optimisation, and information fusion.

Machine Learning: Machine learning is a type of AI algorithm that allows machines to learn from data without being explicitly programmed. It involves training a model on a large dataset and using statistical methods to identify patterns and relationships in the data. The model can then be used to make predictions or decisions based on new data.

There are several types of machines learning algorithms, including supervised learning, unsupervised learning, and reinforcement learning. **Supervised learning** involves training a model on a labelled dataset, where the output is known. The model can then be used to predict the output for new data. **Unsupervised learning**, on the other hand, involves training a model on an unlabelled dataset, where the output is unknown. The model is then used to identify patterns and relationships in the data. **Reinforcement learning** involves training a model to make decisions based on feedback from its environment.

Optimisation: Optimisation algorithms are used to find the optimal solution to a problem, such as minimising costs or maximising profits. These algorithms use mathematical/statistical techniques to search for the best possible solution, given a set of constraints.

There are several types of optimisation algorithms, including **linear programming**, **integer programming**, and **nonlinear programming**. Linear programming involves optimising a linear objective function subject to linear constraints. Integer programming involves optimising a linear objective function subject to integer constraints. Nonlinear programming involves optimising a nonlinear objective function subject to nonlinear constraints.

Information Fusion: Information fusion algorithms are used to combine data from multiple sources to make better predictions or decisions. These algorithms use statistical methods to integrate data from different sources and reduce uncertainty.

There are several types of information fusion algorithms, including **Bayesian networks**, **Dempster-Shafer theory**, and **Fuzzy Logic**. Bayesian networks involve modelling the relationships between variables using probability theory. Dempster-Shafer theory involves combining evidence from multiple sources using belief functions. Fuzzy logic involves modelling uncertainty using fuzzy sets.

2.2 How AI Algorithms Work and Potential Applications?

AI algorithms work by processing and analysing data to identify patterns and relationships. They use mathematical models to learn from the data and make predictions or decisions based on what they have learned. The process of training an AI algorithm involves feeding it a large dataset and adjusting the model parameters to minimise the error between the predicted output and the actual output.

Once the model has been trained, it can be used to make predictions or decisions based on new data. For example, a machine learning model could be trained on a dataset of medical images and used to predict whether a new image contains a tumour. An optimisation algorithm could be used to optimise the scheduling of a workforce to minimise costs. An information fusion algorithm could be used to combine data from multiple sensors to track the movement of a vehicle.

The training process involves feeding the algorithm with data and adjusting its parameters until it produces the desired output. Once the algorithm is trained, it can be used to make predictions or decisions on new data. In conclusion, the different AI algorithms, including machine learning, optimisation, and information fusion, are powerful tools that can be used to solve complex problems and improve decision-making. Understanding the fundamentals of AI is essential for anyone interested in this field.

Information Fusion Algorithms:

Information fusion algorithms, such as Fuzzy Logic, are designed to combine data from multiple sources and produce meaningful insights or make informed decisions based on the aggregated information. Fuzzy Logic, in particular, is a mathematical framework that deals with the representation and manipulation of uncertain or imprecise information.
Fuzzy Logic works by extending the traditional binary logic (which deals with true or false values) to include a continuum of truth values between 0 and 1. This allows for more

nuanced reasoning and decision-making in situations where the information is not clear-cut or where human-like reasoning is required.

An overview of how Fuzzy Logic works:

- Fuzzification: The input data or variables are converted into fuzzy sets, which are characterized by membership functions. Membership functions are used to define the degree of membership of each element in the input data to the fuzzy set, with values ranging between 0 (no membership) and 1 (full membership).

- Rule evaluation: Fuzzy rules are defined to describe the relationship between input fuzzy sets and output fuzzy sets. These rules are usually expressed in the form of IF-THEN statements, such as ***"IF temperature is hot AND humidity is high, THEN air conditioning is on."*** The rules are evaluated based on the input fuzzy sets and their membership values, resulting in the activation of corresponding output fuzzy sets.

- Aggregation: The results of all rule evaluations are combined or aggregated to form a single fuzzy set for each output variable. This is typically done using operators like the maximum or minimum, depending on the problem at hand.

- Defuzzification: The aggregated fuzzy output sets are converted back into crisp values (i.e., specific numerical values) using defuzzification techniques. One common defuzzification method is the centroid method, which calculates the centre of gravity of the aggregated fuzzy set to obtain a single crisp value.

Fuzzy logic is particularly useful in applications where data is noisy, uncertain, or subjective. Examples of such applications include control systems, pattern recognition, decision-making, and natural language processing.

Examples of applications of fusion algorithms:

- Sensor fusion: In robotics and autonomous vehicles, sensor fusion algorithms integrate data from multiple sensors, such as cameras, LIDAR, radar, and GPS, to create a more accurate and robust perception of the environment. This fusion helps improve navigation, obstacle detection, and tracking, enabling safer and more efficient operation.

- Medical imaging: Fusion algorithms are used to combine images from different modalities, such as MRI, CT, and PET scans, to create a more comprehensive view of a patient's anatomy and physiology. This fusion can aid in more accurate diagnosis, treatment planning, and monitoring of diseases.

- Military applications: In defence and intelligence systems, data fusion algorithms integrate information from multiple sources, such as satellite imagery, radar, and ground-based sensors, to improve situational awareness, target tracking, and threat assessment.

- Social media analysis: Fusion algorithms can be employed to aggregate and analyse data from multiple social media platforms, such as Twitter, Facebook, and Instagram, to identify trends, sentiments, or influencers, enabling more effective marketing campaigns or crisis management.

- Financial data fusion: In finance, fusion algorithms can combine data from various sources, such as stock prices, financial statements, and economic indicators, to create more accurate forecasts, risk assessments, and investment strategies.

- Multimodal biometrics: In biometric authentication systems, fusion algorithms can integrate data from multiple biometric modalities, such as fingerprint, facial, and voice recognition, to enhance the accuracy and robustness of the authentication process.

- Remote sensing: In earth observation and environmental monitoring, fusion algorithms can be used to merge data from different satellite sensors, such as optical, radar, and hyperspectral imagery, to create more accurate land cover maps, monitor vegetation health, or detect changes in land use.

These examples demonstrate the versatility of fusion algorithms in integrating and processing data from multiple sources across various domains, from robotics and medical imaging to finance and defence. The choice of the fusion algorithm depends on the nature of the problem, the characteristics of the data, and the desired level of integration, which can range from low-level (data or feature fusion) to high-level (decision or model fusion).

An example of how an information fusion algorithm works: Figure 21 illustrates a straightforward example of how a fusion algorithm operates. Imagine a basket filled with various fruits, and our task is to identify a mango or an orange among them. To accomplish this, we employ a set of if-then rules based on characteristics such as colour, texture, size, and shape, and then integrate these rules to pinpoint the desired fruit. This method mirrors the approach commonly used in everyday decision-making processes. For instance, doctors diagnose illnesses by evaluating symptoms through a similar set of rules, chefs follow specific guidelines when preparing dishes, and decision-makers apply analogous methods to reach their conclusions.

This example not only demonstrates the functionality of a fusion algorithm but also highlights its relevance and application in routine activities.

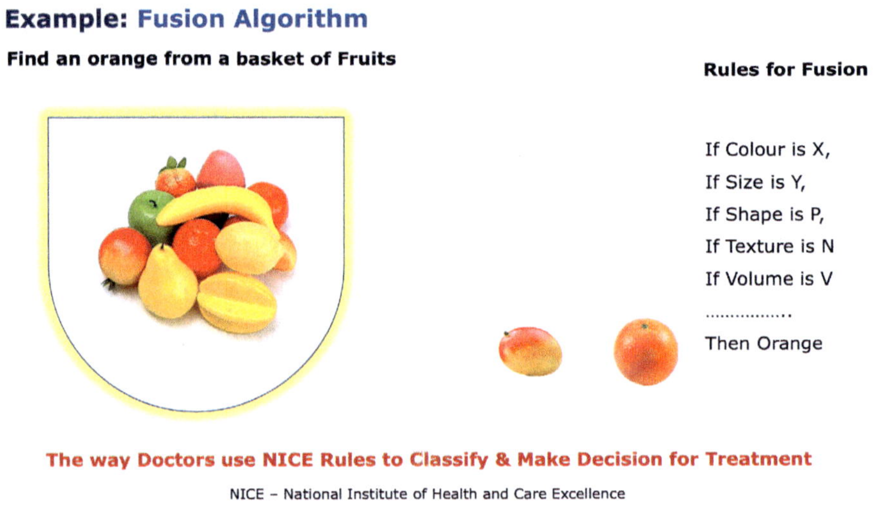

Figure 2.1 Example of Fusion

Machine Learning Algorithms:

Machine learning algorithms enable computers to learn patterns and make decisions from data without being explicitly programmed. They typically work by constructing a model that can generalise from a training dataset to make predictions or decisions on new, unseen data. Deep learning, a subfield of machine learning, focuses on using deep neural networks to learn complex patterns and representations.

Here's a step-by-step overview of how machine learning algorithms work, with an example of deep learning:

- Data collection and pre-processing: Collect a dataset containing examples with relevant features and, if applicable, target labels. For instance, in a deep learning image classification task, the dataset would consist of labelled images. Pre-process the data to remove noise, handle missing values, and normalise or scale the features. This step is crucial for improving the performance and accuracy of the algorithm.

- Feature extraction and selection: Features are the measurable properties or characteristics of the data that can be used for learning and prediction. In deep learning, the neural network automatically learns and extracts relevant features from raw data, such as identifying edges or shapes in images.

- Model selection: Choose an appropriate machine learning algorithm or model based on the problem type (e.g., regression, classification, clustering) and the characteristics of the data. In the case of deep learning, a deep neural network architecture is selected, comprising multiple layers of interconnected artificial neurons or nodes.

- Model training: Train the model using the training dataset. In deep learning, the neural network learns the optimal weights and biases by iteratively adjusting them to minimise a loss function. The loss function quantifies the difference between the model's predictions and the actual target values. This process typically involves forward propagation, loss calculation, backpropagation, and weight update using an optimisation algorithm like gradient descent or a variant such as Adam or RMSprop.

- Model evaluation and validation: Evaluate the trained model on a separate dataset (validation or test set) to assess its performance on unseen data. Common performance metrics include accuracy, precision, recall, and F1 score for classification tasks, and mean squared error or mean absolute error for regression tasks. This step helps to ensure that the model generalises well and does not overfit or underfit the training data.

- Hyperparameter tuning: Adjust the model's hyperparameters (e.g., learning rate, network architecture, activation functions) and retrain the model to improve its performance based on the evaluation results. Techniques like grid search, random search, and Bayesian optimization can be employed for systematic hyperparameter tuning.

- Model deployment: Once the model has been trained, evaluated, and fine-tuned, it can be deployed in a production environment to make predictions or decisions on new, unseen data.

For example, in a deep learning image classification task, a convolutional neural network (CNN) could be employed to identify objects within images. ***The CNN would learn to recognize patterns and features within the images during the training phase, adjusting its weights and biases to minimize the loss function.*** After training and evaluation, the CNN can be used to classify new, unlabelled images, predicting the objects they contain with high accuracy.

Examples of applications of machine learning algorithms:

- Spam detection: Machine learning algorithms like Naive Bayes, Support Vector Machines, or Random Forest can be used to automatically classify emails as spam or not spam based on features such as the sender, subject line, and email content.
- Image recognition: Convolutional Neural Networks (CNNs), a type of deep learning algorithm, can be used to identify and classify objects in images, enabling applications like facial recognition, self-driving cars, or medical image analysis.

- Natural language processing (NLP): Machine learning algorithms like Recurrent Neural Networks (RNNs), Long Short-Term Memory (LSTM) networks, or Transformers can be used to process and analyse human language for applications such as sentiment analysis, language translation, or chatbots.
- Fraud detection: Machine learning algorithms like Logistic Regression, Decision Trees, or Neural Networks can be employed to detect fraudulent transactions in banking or insurance by analysing patterns and anomalies in transaction data.
- Recommendation systems: Collaborative filtering and content-based filtering algorithms can be used to create personalised recommendations for users in e-commerce, streaming services, or social media platforms based on their browsing history, preferences, and behaviour.
- Anomaly detection: Machine learning algorithms like k-Nearest Neighbours, One-Class Support Vector Machines, or Autoencoders can be used to identify unusual patterns or outliers in data, which can be useful in applications such as network security, quality control, or fault detection.
- Customer segmentation: Unsupervised machine learning algorithms like k-means clustering or hierarchical clustering can be used to group customers based on their

behaviour, preferences, or demographics, enabling targeted marketing campaigns or personalised customer experiences.

- Predictive maintenance: Machine learning algorithms like Regression, Random Forest, or Gradient Boosting can be employed to predict equipment failures or maintenance requirements based on historical sensor data, reducing downtime and maintenance costs.

These examples demonstrate the versatility of machine learning algorithms in solving a wide range of real-world problems across various domains, from NLP and computer vision to finance and customer analytics. The choice of the machine learning algorithm depends on the nature of the problem, the characteristics of the data, and the desired outcome or performance metric.

<u>An example of how a machine learning algorithm works</u>**:** Figure 2.2 provides a clear depiction of the workings of a supervised machine learning algorithm. The first step involves training the algorithm with a substantial dataset and existing knowledge. Specifically, as shown in Figure 2.2, the algorithm is trained to recognize various skin diseases. Once the training phase is complete, the algorithm becomes capable of identifying new instances of skin diseases, provided they are similar to the data (in this case, images) used during

training. It's important to note that the accuracy and effectiveness of the algorithm heavily depend on the quality and volume of the data and knowledge it was trained with. Insufficient or poor-quality data can lead to inaccurate results, underscoring the importance of a robust training dataset for reliable algorithm performance.

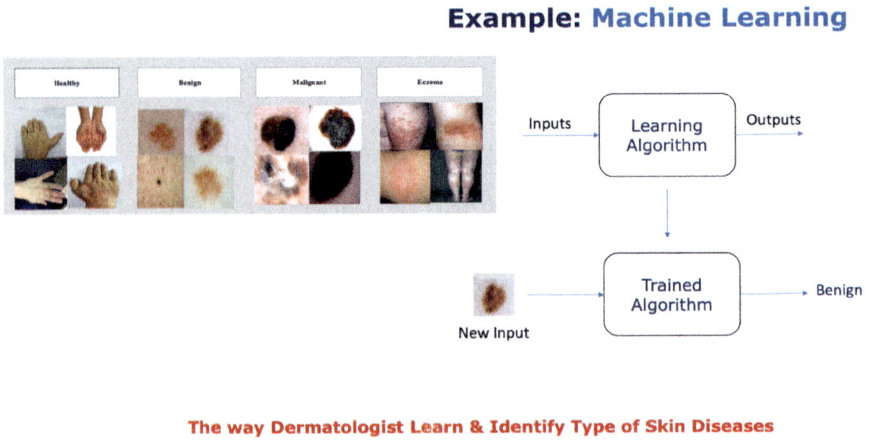

Figure 2.2: How machine learning algorithm work

Optimisation Algorithms and Applications:

While all optimisation algorithms share the common goal of finding the best possible solution to a given problem, they do not all work in the same way. Different optimisation algorithms employ various techniques to explore the solution space and iteratively improve the candidate solutions based on the objective function.

Here are some categories of optimisation algorithms and their distinctive approaches:

- Gradient-based methods (e.g., Gradient Descent, Conjugate Gradient, Newton's method): These methods rely on the calculation of gradients (partial derivatives) of the objective function with respect to the decision variables. They use the gradient information to determine the direction and step size for updating the candidate solution iteratively, aiming to minimize (or maximize) the objective function.

- Metaheuristic algorithms (e.g., Genetic Algorithm, Particle Swarm Optimization, Ant Colony Optimisation): These are stochastic optimisation methods inspired by natural or social phenomena. They work by maintaining a population of candidate solutions and applying search operators such as selection, crossover, mutation, or local search to explore and exploit the solution space.

- Linear and Integer Programming (e.g., Simplex method, Branch and Bound): These methods are designed for problems with linear objective functions and constraints. They work by iteratively refining the candidate solution using techniques like matrix manipulation, cutting planes, or branching strategies to find the optimal solution within a feasible region.

- Direct search methods (e.g., Nelder-Mead, Hooke-Jeeves): These methods do not require gradient information and typically rely on comparisons of objective function values to guide the search. They work by iteratively updating the candidate solution using geometric transformations or pattern searches.

- Bayesian optimisation: This is a global optimisation technique based on probabilistic modelling and acquisition functions. It works by constructing a surrogate model (e.g., Gaussian Process) of the objective function and iteratively updating the model based on new samples, chosen to maximise an acquisition function that balances exploration and exploitation.

- Simulated Annealing: This is a stochastic optimisation method inspired by the annealing process in metallurgy. It works by exploring the solution space using random perturbations, accepting, or rejecting new solutions based on a probability function that depends on the objective function and a temperature parameter, which decreases over time.

These categories exemplify the diverse techniques employed by optimization algorithms. While some methods may share similarities, the specific workings of each algorithm can vary significantly.

The choice of an optimisation algorithm depends on factors such as the nature of the problem, the objective function, the available information (e.g., gradient), and the computational constraints.

An example of how optimization algorithms work using the Gradient Descent technique, which is commonly used in machine learning:

Problem: Suppose we have a dataset with several data points and want to find the best-fitting straight line (linear regression) that minimises the error between the predicted values and the actual values. In this case, the objective function is the mean squared error (MSE), which measures the average squared difference between the predicted and actual values.

Step-by-step process of Gradient Descent:

- Initialisation: Choose an initial set of values for the model parameters, which, in this case, are the slope (m) and the intercept (b) of the straight line.

- Compute the objective function: Calculate the mean squared error (MSE) for the current values of m and b, considering the given data points.

- Calculate the gradients: Compute the partial derivatives of the MSE with respect to m and b. These gradients indicate the direction and magnitude of change required to reduce the error.

- Update the parameters: Update the values of m and b by subtracting the gradients multiplied by a learning rate (a small positive constant). The learning rate controls the step size of the updates and ensures that the optimization process converges smoothly.

- Iterate: Repeat steps 2-4 for a predetermined number of iterations or until a convergence criterion is met, such as a minimal change in the objective function or reaching a maximum number of iterations.

- Optimal solution: Once the algorithm converges, the final values of m and b represent the best-fitting straight line that minimizes the mean squared error.

In summary, optimisation algorithms work by iteratively updating the candidate solutions based on the objective function to find the best possible solution for a given problem. The example provided illustrates the Gradient Descent optimization algorithm in the context of linear regression, where the goal is to find the best-fitting straight line that minimizes the mean squared error between the predicted and actual values.

Examples of applications of optimisation algorithms:

- Machine learning: In supervised learning, optimisation algorithms like Gradient Descent or Quasi-Newton methods are used to find the best model parameters that minimise a loss function, such as mean squared error for regression tasks or cross-entropy loss for classification tasks.

- Supply chain management: Optimisation algorithms like Linear Programming or Mixed Integer Programming can be used to minimise costs, maximise profits, or optimise resource allocation in various supply chain processes such as production planning, transportation, and inventory management.

- Vehicle routing: In logistics, the Vehicle Routing Problem (VRP) involves determining optimal routes for a fleet of vehicles to deliver goods to customers. Optimisation algorithms like Branch and Bound, Genetic Algorithm, or Ant Colony Optimisation can be used to minimise the total distance travelled, fuel consumption, or delivery time.

- Image processing: In image segmentation or object recognition tasks, optimisation algorithms like Graph Cuts or Simulated Annealing can be used to find the best segmentation or object boundaries that minimise an energy function, which measures the quality of the segmentation or recognition.

- Portfolio optimisation: In finance, optimisation algorithms like Quadratic Programming or Particle Swarm Optimisation can be employed to find the optimal portfolio allocation that maximises returns and minimizes risks, based on historical data and constraints such as budget or diversification requirements.

- Traveling Salesman Problem (TSP): In TSP, the objective is to find the shortest possible route that visits a given set of cities and returns to the starting city. Optimisation algorithms like Branch and Bound, Simulated Annealing, or Genetic Algorithm can be employed to find approximate or optimal solutions to the problem.

- Structural optimisation: In engineering, optimisation algorithms like Genetic Algorithm, Particle Swarm Optimisation, or Gradient-Based methods can be used to minimise the weight or material usage in structures such as bridges, buildings, or aircraft while meeting performance and safety constraints.

These examples demonstrate the versatility of optimisation algorithms in solving a wide range of real-world problems across various domains, from machine learning and finance to logistics and engineering. ***The choice of the optimisation algorithm depends on the nature of the problem, the objective function, and the constraints imposed on the solution space.***

<u>An example of how an optimisation algorithm works</u>: Figure 2.3 effectively demonstrates the application of optimisation in real-world scenarios. Take, for instance, the task of selecting the most efficient driving route from one location to another. This decision involves considering a multitude of factors, such as current traffic conditions, distance, road quality, and time. Additionally, personal preferences or comfort levels may also influence the choice of route. The complexity of balancing these various parameters makes it challenging for humans to identify the optimal route unaided. This is where navigation tools come into play, assisting in making well-informed decisions. It's noteworthy that the human brain often struggles with decision-making when faced with more than two variables. In such situations, AI optimization algorithms can be particularly beneficial, adeptly handling multiple parameters to determine the best possible outcome.

Figure 2.3: Example of how optimisation algorithm works.

2.3 Data-Driven Decision Support Systems

In a wide array of real-world scenarios, data-driven Decision Support Systems (DSS) play a pivotal role in facilitating the decision-making process. These systems, regardless of the domain—be it health, education, agriculture, or business—follow a universal framework. This framework typically integrates hybrid AI algorithms, encompassing machine learning, optimization, and fusion techniques, for effective monitoring, prediction, and decision-making.

Figure 2.4 provides a clear illustration of this framework, specifically tailored for health applications. However, the versatility of the model allows for its adaptation across various domains. Within this framework, machine learning algorithms are employed to extract knowledge from existing datasets. This extracted knowledge is then validated and refined in consultation with domain experts. The resulting knowledge model becomes a crucial tool for analysing new inputs, enabling the system to contextualize and interpret fresh data in light of the accumulated knowledge.

Further, the framework utilizes information fusion for continuous monitoring and predictive analysis. In situations where multiple decision-making options are available, optimisation techniques are applied to distinguish the most effective decision from a range of possibilities. It's important to note that the necessity and complexity of the algorithms employed are contingent upon the complexity of the problem at hand. This adaptive approach ensures that the data driven DSS remains both efficient and relevant across different applications and challenges.

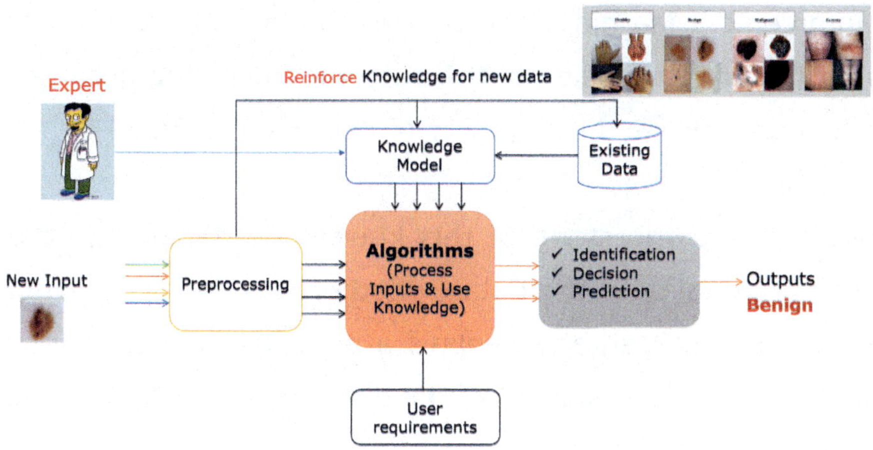

Figure 2.4: Framework of data driven DSS

Steps of generating knowledge from data

The process of transforming data into knowledge involves several critical steps, as depicted in Figure 2.5. These steps include data collection, pre-processing, feature extraction, and processing. Each stage encompasses a variety of methods, analyses, and evaluations. AI algorithms play an essential role in executing many of these tasks, such as reconstruction, classification, clustering, and prediction.

The selection of the appropriate AI algorithm(s) is a crucial task for AI engineers, tailored to the specific needs of the project. This selection process is intricate, as an incorrect choice can lead to suboptimal or unreliable performance. The challenge lies in the vast array of available options, ranging from basic machine learning techniques like neural networks to more advanced approaches such as deep learning or deep reinforcement learning. The choice of algorithm significantly impacts various aspects of the outcome, including accuracy, execution time, and the quality of decision-making.

Data is the cornerstone of this knowledge generation process. The quality of the data—whether it is sufficient, unbiased, and representative—plays a vital role in determining the accuracy and reliability of the derived knowledge. Therefore, careful consideration must be given to ethical data collection methods, formats, reconstruction, and filtering. Any shortcomings in the data can have cascading effects across different layers of analysis and the resulting knowledge models. For instance, biases in data regarding age groups can lead to discriminatory decisions affecting other age groups.

In summary, the journey from data to knowledge is a complex and multi-faceted process, heavily reliant on the judicious selection of AI algorithms and the integrity of the data used. Ensuring both these elements are appropriately addressed is crucial for the successful application of data-driven knowledge in any field.

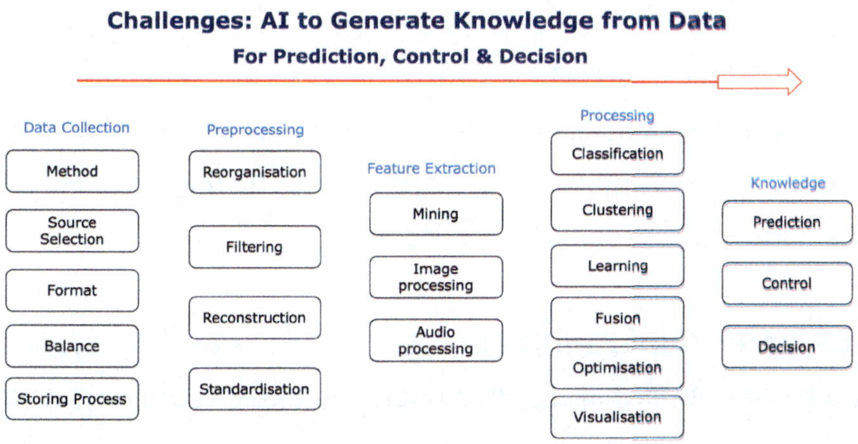

Figure 2.5: Steps of generating knowledge from data

2.4 Risks of AI Systems

Despite their considerable potential, AI systems are accompanied by a range of risks, encompassing technical aspects (both software and hardware), ethical concerns, and legal compliance challenges. A brief overview of these risks is provided below:

Software Risks:

Algorithmic Bias: AI algorithms can inadvertently perpetuate and amplify biases present in their training data. This can lead to unfair or discriminatory outcomes, especially in sensitive applications like hiring, lending, and law enforcement.

Data Privacy and Security: AI systems often require access to large datasets, which can include sensitive personal information. There's a risk of data breaches or misuse, leading to privacy violations.

Dependence on Data Quality: The effectiveness of AI is heavily dependent on the quality of the data used for training. Poor, incomplete, or unrepresentative data can lead to inaccurate or unreliable AI outputs.

Software Vulnerabilities: Like any software, AI systems can have vulnerabilities that might be exploited by cyber attackers, potentially leading to system failures or data breaches.

Unpredictability and Lack of Explainability: Some AI models, particularly deep learning systems, can be "black boxes," offering little insight into how they reach conclusions. This lack of transparency can be risky in critical applications.

Hardware Risks:

Physical Failures: AI systems, especially those in robotics or autonomous vehicles, rely on hardware that can fail, leading to physical accidents or system malfunctions.

Dependence on Hardware Performance: The efficiency and capability of AI systems are often tied to hardware performance. Limitations in processing power or memory can constrain AI effectiveness.

Environmental Impact: The hardware required for training and running sophisticated AI models, particularly data centres, can have a significant environmental footprint, contributing to energy consumption and carbon emissions.

Supply Chain Vulnerabilities: AI hardware components can be subject to supply chain disruptions, which can impact the availability and cost of AI technologies.

Ethical Issues:

Job Displacement: Automation through AI could lead to job displacement in certain sectors, raising concerns about employment and economic inequality.

Manipulation and Control: AI can be used to manipulate user behaviour or spread misinformation, raising ethical concerns about autonomy and consent.

Surveillance and Privacy: The use of AI in surveillance technologies can lead to over-monitoring and infringe on individual privacy rights.

Moral and Human Rights Concerns: Decisions made by AI systems, especially in critical areas like healthcare or criminal justice, raise profound moral and human rights concerns.

Legal Compliance:

Regulatory Compliance: As AI regulation evolves, there's a risk of non-compliance with new or existing laws, especially in areas like data protection (GDPR) and consumer rights.

Liability and Accountability: Determining liability in cases where AI systems cause harm or make erroneous decisions can be complex, raising legal challenges.

Intellectual Property Issues: AI can generate content or inventions, leading to legal questions about ownership and intellectual property rights.

Cross-Border Data Flow: AI systems often involve cross-border data flows, which can be subject to varying regulations in different jurisdictions, complicating compliance efforts.

Contractual Risks: AI can impact contractual obligations, especially where performance is dependent on AI accuracy or reliability.

In summary, while AI offers transformative potential, it also brings a range of risks that need careful management across software, hardware, ethical, and legal dimensions. Addressing these risks requires a multi-faceted approach involving robust design and testing, ethical considerations, and compliance with evolving legal standards.

Chapter 3:

AI, ChatGPT & Other LLMS for Business

3.1 ChatGPT and Other Language Models for Businesses

What is ChatGPT?

ChatGPT is an advanced language model based on the GPT-3.5 architecture developed by OpenAI. It stands for "Chat Generative Pretrained Transformer" and represents one of the most sophisticated AI language models available. Built upon deep learning principles, ChatGPT excels at understanding and generating human-like text, making it capable of engaging in meaningful conversations with users. This transformative technology has the potential to revolutionise how businesses interact with customers, automate tasks, and make better decisions.

How ChatGPT Works?

ChatGPT's working mechanism is divided into two key phases: pre-training and fine-tuning. During pre-training, the model is exposed to an extensive dataset containing a vast amount of diverse text from the internet. This process helps ChatGPT to learn linguistic patterns, grammar rules, and general knowledge about the world. Consequently, the model acquires a broad understanding of human language.

After pre-training, the model undergoes fine-tuning. This stage refines the model's capabilities for specific tasks by exposing it to more targeted datasets. Fine-tuning allows ChatGPT to specialise in particular domains, such as customer service, marketing, or product recommendations. The fine-tuning process involves using reinforcement learning and human feedback to enhance the model's responses and ensure it aligns with business requirements.

Importance and Applications of ChatGPT:

The importance of ChatGPT for businesses cannot be overstated. It opens up new avenues for automation, customer engagement, and decision-making. With ChatGPT, businesses can enhance their customer service, streamline communication, and improve overall operational efficiency. Moreover, the model's ability to process and analyse vast amounts of data enables better insights, leading to data-driven strategies and decision-making.

Some applications of ChatGPT in Businesses:

Customer Support and Service: ChatGPT can be deployed as a virtual assistant to handle customer queries, providing instant responses, and resolving common issues. By automating customer support, businesses can ensure 24/7 availability and reduce response times, thereby enhancing customer satisfaction.

Marketing and Personalisation: Using ChatGPT, businesses can craft personalised marketing campaigns and targeted advertisements. The model can analyse user data, preferences, and behaviour to deliver tailored recommendations and promotions, resulting in higher engagement and conversions.

Content Generation: ChatGPT's natural language generation abilities make it a valuable tool for content creation. Businesses can utilise the model to generate blog posts, social media content, product descriptions, and more, saving time and resources in content production.

Decision Support: With its analytical capabilities, ChatGPT can assist businesses in making informed decisions. By processing and interpreting complex data sets, the model can provide insights and recommendations that aid in strategic planning, resource allocation, and risk assessment.

Overall, ChatGPT represents a significant advancement in AI language models, offering businesses unprecedented opportunities to optimize operations, elevate customer experiences, and foster data-driven decision-making. Through its advanced algorithms and natural language processing, ChatGPT enables businesses to engage with customers more effectively, generate personalised content, and leverage data-driven insights to stay competitive in today's dynamic market landscape. As this technology continues to evolve, it holds the promise of even more transformative applications, empowering businesses to unlock new levels of efficiency and innovation.

BloombergGPT Model for Businesses:

BloombergGPT is a large language model (LLM) developed by Bloomberg. It is a 50-billion parameter model that is trained on a massive dataset of financial data. This data includes news articles, financial statements, and research reports. BloombergGPT is able to perform a variety of financial tasks, such as:

Sentiment analysis: BloombergGPT can be used to analyse the sentiment of financial news articles and other text. This information can be used to identify potential investment opportunities or risks.

Named entity recognition: BloombergGPT can identify named entities in financial text, such as companies, countries, and currencies. This information can be used to track the performance of companies and to identify trends in the market.

Question answering: BloombergGPT can answer questions about financial data. This information can be used to make investment decisions or to learn more about the financial markets.

By making it easier to understand and analyse financial data, BloombergGPT can help people make better investment decisions and to stay ahead of the market.

Other Language Models for Businesses:

Apart from the above two models, several other language models have proven to be useful for businesses in various capacities. These models, developed by different organisations, offer a range of functionalities from natural language processing to complex data analysis. Some notable examples include:

BERT (Bidirectional Encoder Representations from Transformers): Developed by Google, BERT is particularly effective in understanding the context of a word in a search query, making it valuable for search engine optimization and content relevance.

T5 (Text-To-Text Transfer Transformer): Also developed by Google, T5 adopts a unique approach by converting all NLP tasks into a text-to-text format. It's useful for summarization, translation, and question-answering tasks.

XLNet: Developed by Google and Carnegie Mellon University, XLNet outperforms BERT in some scenarios by learning the permutation of the sequence of words, rather than just the sequence itself. This makes it particularly effective for tasks requiring a deep understanding of context.

RoBERTa (Robustly Optimised BERT Pretraining Approach): Developed by Facebook AI, RoBERTa is an optimized version of BERT, designed to improve its performance. It's widely used in sentiment analysis and content classification.

ERNIE (Enhanced Representation through kNowledge Integration): Developed by Baidu, ERNIE is designed to better understand the nuances of language by integrating knowledge graphs into training, making it effective for tasks that require a deep understanding of context and semantics.

DistilBERT: A streamlined version of BERT, DistilBERT offers a balance between performance and resource efficiency, making it suitable for businesses looking for cost-effective NLP solutions.

ELECTRA: Developed by Google, ELECTRA is designed to be more efficient than models like BERT, making it suitable for businesses with limited computational resources.

OpenAI Codex: Also, from OpenAI, Codex is particularly adept at understanding and generating programming code, making it useful for businesses involved in software development and coding education.

Each of these models has its strengths and is suited to different business needs, from enhancing customer interaction to automating content creation and improving search engine optimization. The choice of model often depends on the specific requirements of the task, such as the complexity of language understanding needed, the volume of data to be processed, and the computational resources available.

3.2 Potential and Challenges of AI and ChatGPT in Businesses

The integration of AI and ChatGPT into the business world has been transformative, with numerous opportunities for streamlining processes, enhancing customer experiences, and driving innovation. As a result, businesses can leverage the potential of AI and ChatGPT to increase efficiency, improve decision-making, and ultimately generate higher profits.

Some of the most significant opportunities offered by AI and ChatGPT in businesses include:

Automation: AI-powered systems can automate repetitive tasks, freeing up employees to focus on higher-value work and reducing human error.

Enhanced customer service: ChatGPT can be employed to create intelligent chatbots and virtual assistants that provide personalised, 24/7 support to customers.

Improved data analysis: AI algorithms can process large volumes of data, offering businesses valuable insights and helping them make data-driven decisions.

Innovation and competitiveness: AI and ChatGPT can drive innovation in product development and customer engagement, giving businesses a competitive edge in the market.

However, the integration of AI and ChatGPT into businesses is not without challenges:

Ethical concerns: The use of AI can raise ethical issues, such as data privacy, algorithmic bias, and the potential for job displacement.

Security risks: The increasing reliance on AI systems can expose businesses to new cybersecurity threats and vulnerabilities.

Technical complexities: Implementing AI and ChatGPT can be complex, requiring specialised knowledge and resources to manage and maintain these systems.

Legal and regulatory compliance: As AI and ChatGPT become more widespread, businesses need to be aware of and comply with evolving legal and regulatory requirements related to their use.

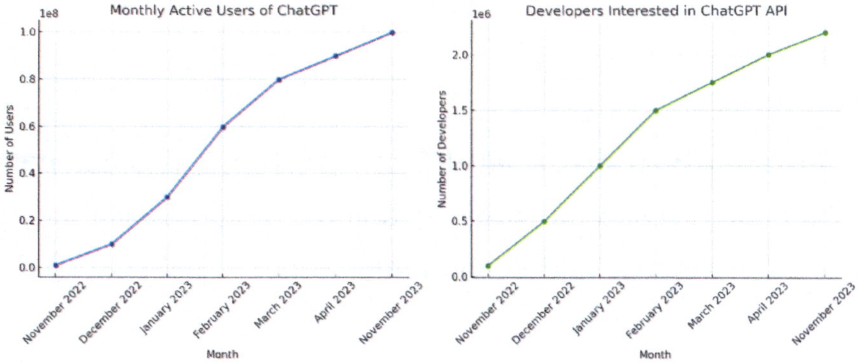

Figure 3.1: Monthly Active Users of ChatGPT and Developers Interested in ChatGPT API

3.3 AI and ChatGPT in Business Operations

Streamlining Customer Service with ChatGPT

One of the most promising applications of ChatGPT in business is the improvement of customer service. By implementing AI-powered chatbots, businesses can provide quick, accurate, and personalised responses to customer inquiries, leading to a better overall customer experience.

Benefits of ChatGPT in customer service include:

- **24/7 availability**: Chatbots can handle customer inquiries around the clock, providing instant support even outside of regular business hours.

- **Cost savings**: Automated customer service can reduce the need for human agents, resulting in cost savings for businesses.

- **Personalisation**: ChatGPT can analyse customer data and preferences to provide tailored responses, making customers feel valued and understood.

- **Scalability**: Chatbots can easily handle increased demand without compromising response times or quality, ensuring a consistently high level of service.

Optimising Supply Chain Management with AI:

AI has the potential to revolutionise supply chain management by automating tasks, improving efficiency, and enabling data-driven decision-making. Some of the ways AI can optimise supply chain management include:

- **Demand forecasting**: AI algorithms can analyse historical data and predict future demand patterns, allowing businesses to optimise inventory levels and reduce the risk of stockouts or overstocking.

- **Route optimisation**: AI can analyse various factors such as traffic, weather, and fuel costs to determine the most efficient routes for transportation and delivery.

- **Supplier selection and monitoring**: AI can evaluate supplier performance based on factors such as cost, quality, and reliability, helping businesses make better decisions regarding supplier partnerships.

- **Risk management**: AI can identify potential risks in the supply chain and suggest appropriate mitigation strategies, enabling businesses to address issues proactively.

Enhancing Decision-Making with AI-Driven Predictive Analytics:

Predictive analytics refers to the use of AI algorithms to analyse historical data, identify patterns, and forecast future outcomes. By leveraging predictive analytics, businesses can make more informed decisions, optimise resources, and improve overall performance. Some applications of predictive analytics in business operations include:

- **Sales and marketing**: AI-driven predictive analytics can help businesses identify customer segments, predict purchasing behaviour, and optimise marketing strategies to increase sales and customer engagement.

- **Human resources**: AI can analyse employee data to predict attrition, identify high-potential talent, and optimise recruitment and retention strategies.

- **Financial management**: Predictive analytics can provide valuable insights into revenue trends, expense management, and risk assessment, enabling businesses to make data-driven financial decisions.

- **Quality control**: AI can analyse production data to identify patterns and anomalies, allowing businesses to predict and prevent defects, improve product quality, and minimise waste.

By harnessing the power of AI in business operations, companies can streamline processes, optimise resources, and ultimately enhance their decision-making capabilities. However, it is crucial for businesses to be mindful of the challenges associated with AI implementation, such as ethical concerns, security risks, and technical complexities, to ensure long-term success.

AI Fraud detection and Credit Risk in Finance:

AI is being used increasingly in the financial industry to detect fraud and assess credit risk. AI-based fraud detection systems can analyse large amounts of data to identify patterns that indicate fraudulent activity. This can help financial institutions to prevent fraud before it happens, or to detect it early on so that it can be stopped quickly.

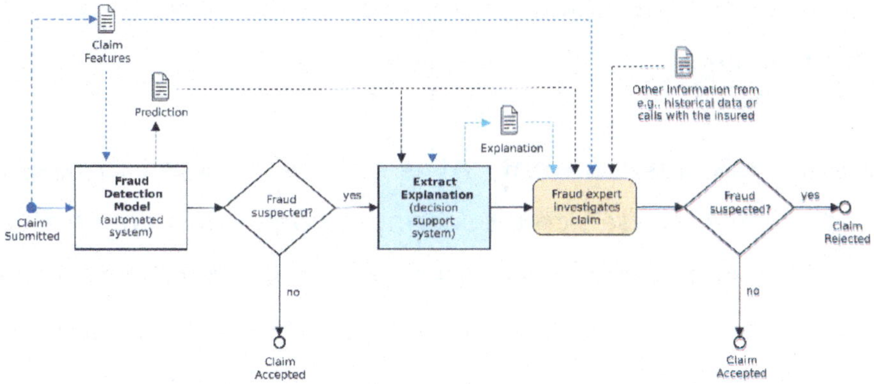

Figure 3.2: Diagram illustrating of how AI is utilised in fraud detection. (Source: See Reading List)

AI is also being used to assess credit risk. AI-based credit scoring models can take into account a wider range of factors than traditional credit scoring models, such as social media activity and online behaviour. This can help financial institutions to make more accurate decisions about who to lend money to.

The ways that AI is being used in fraud detection and credit risk in finance are as follows:

Fraud detection: AI-based fraud detection systems can analyse large amounts of data to identify patterns that indicate fraudulent activity. This can help financial institutions to prevent fraud before it happens, or to detect it early on so that it can be stopped quickly. For example, AI-based fraud detection systems can be used to identify fraudulent credit card transactions, fraudulent insurance claims, and fraudulent wire transfers.

Credit risk assessment: AI is also being used to assess credit risk. AI-based credit scoring models can take into account a wider range of factors than traditional credit scoring models, such as social media activity and online behaviour. This can help financial institutions to make more accurate decisions about who to lend money to. For example, AI-based credit scoring models can be used to assess the risk of default for a loan applicant.

AI is a relatively new technology, but it has the potential to revolutionise the way that fraud detection and credit risk are managed in the financial industry. By using AI, financial institutions can improve their ability to prevent fraud, assess credit risk, and make better lending decisions.

Some of the benefits of using AI for fraud detection and credit risk are as follows:

Increased accuracy: AI-based systems are more accurate than traditional fraud detection and credit risk assessment methods. This is because AI systems can analyse large amounts of data and identify patterns that would be missed by human analysts.

Reduced costs: AI-based systems can help financial institutions to reduce the costs of fraud detection and credit risk assessment. This is because AI systems can automate many of the tasks that are currently performed by human analysts.

Improved customer experience: AI-based systems can help financial institutions to improve the customer experience. This is because AI systems can detect fraud and assess credit risk more quickly and accurately than human analysts. This can help financial institutions to resolve fraud cases more quickly and to approve loans more quickly.

Overall, AI has the potential to revolutionise the way that fraud detection and credit risk are managed in the financial industry. By using AI, financial institutions can improve their ability to prevent fraud, assess credit risk, and make better lending decisions.

3.4 AI and ChatGPT in Marketing

Personalising Customer Experiences with AI:

One of the key advantages of implementing AI in marketing is the ability to personalise customer experiences. Businesses can leverage AI algorithms to analyse customer behaviour, preferences, and purchase history to deliver tailored product recommendations and promotional offers. This personalised approach results in higher customer satisfaction and increased brand loyalty, as customers feel that their unique needs and interests are being met.

Furthermore, AI-powered chatbots like ChatGPT can handle customer service tasks, providing quick and efficient assistance to customers, while also gathering valuable data on their preferences and concerns. This data can be used to further refine marketing strategies and tailor communication to each individual customer.

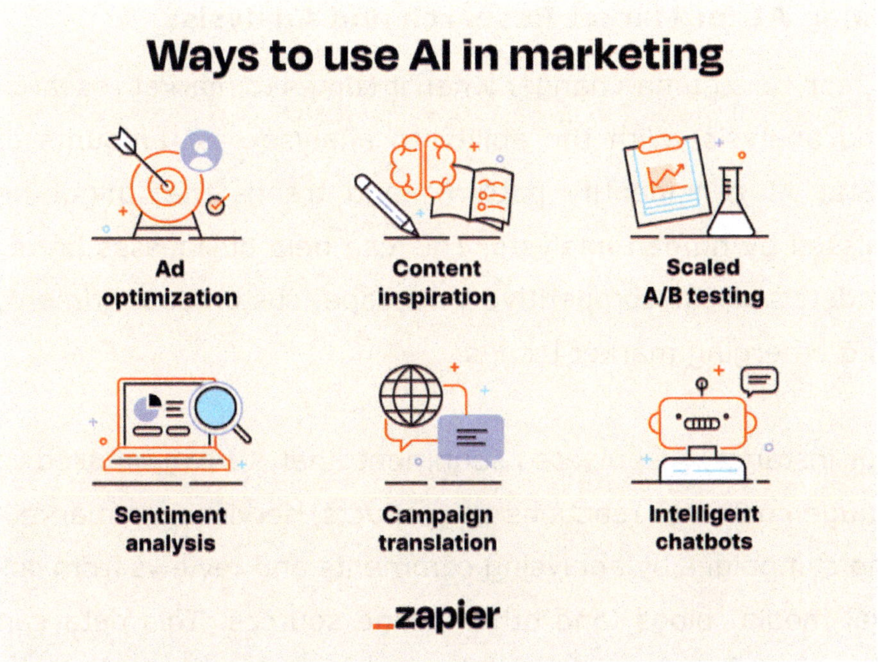

Figure 3.3 AI in marketing (Source: See Reading List)

Automating Marketing Campaigns with ChatGPT:

ChatGPT, as a powerful natural language processing tool, has the potential to revolutionise the way businesses approach marketing campaigns. By automating the creation of marketing content, such as ad copy, social media posts, and email newsletters, ChatGPT can streamline marketing efforts and save businesses valuable time and resources.

Moreover, ChatGPT's ability to understand and generate human-like text enables it to produce content that is both engaging and contextually relevant. This, in turn, improves conversion rates and ensures that marketing messages resonate with the target audience.

Using AI for Market Research and Analysis:

AI can be a game-changer when it comes to market research and analysis. With the ability to analyse vast amounts of data, AI can identify patterns and trends that might be missed by human analysts. This can help businesses better understand the competitive landscape, customer sentiment, and emerging market trends.

For instance, AI-powered sentiment analysis can be used to gauge customer reactions to products, services, or marketing campaigns by analysing comments and reviews from social media, blogs, and other online sources. This data can then be used to adjust marketing strategies or address customer concerns proactively.

In summary, AI and ChatGPT offer numerous opportunities for businesses to improve their marketing efforts. By personalising customer experiences, automating marketing campaigns, and conducting market research and analysis, businesses can enhance customer satisfaction, streamline marketing efforts, and stay ahead of the competition. However, it is important to remember that the implementation of AI and ChatGPT comes with its own set of challenges, such as data privacy concerns and the need for a skilled workforce to manage and maintain these technologies.

Using AI to Generate Videos and Images:

The advent of Artificial Intelligence (AI) in the field of marketing has revolutionised how businesses engage with their audience. AI-driven image and video generation is at the forefront of this revolution, offering innovative, efficient, and highly personalised ways to create marketing content.

Figure 3.4: Images Created by AI with Simple questions:
Create a visual 3D model of the human body with blood circulation.
Create a housing model with a nice river view beside the house.

Capabilities of AI in Image and Video Generation:

- **Personalisation:** AI can analyse customer data to create tailored images and videos that resonate with individual preferences, significantly enhancing customer engagement.
- **Efficiency and Scalability:** With AI, the generation of high-quality visual content can be automated, allowing to produce large volumes of marketing materials in a fraction of the time it would take manually.

- **Consistency in Branding:** AI algorithms can be trained to adhere to specific brand guidelines, ensuring consistency in style, tone, and messaging across all marketing materials.
- **Innovative Content Creation:** AI can generate unique and creative images and videos that might not be feasible with traditional methods, opening new avenues for innovative marketing campaigns.

Applications in Marketing:

- **Social Media Campaigns:** AI-generated visuals can be used to create eye-catching and engaging posts tailored for different platforms and target audiences.
- **Email Marketing:** Personalized images and videos in emails can significantly improve open and click-through rates, as they cater to the specific interests of the recipients.
- **Advertising:** AI can create a variety of ad creatives for A/B testing, quickly identifying which visuals perform best with different demographics.
- **E-commerce:** Product images and demonstration videos can be automatically generated to showcase products in a variety of settings, appealing to a broader range of customers.

Ethical Considerations and Challenges:

- **Transparency:** It's essential for marketers to disclose the use of AI-generated content to maintain trust and authenticity with their audience.

- **Quality Control:** While AI can produce content quickly, human oversight is necessary to ensure that the generated images and videos meet quality standards and are appropriate for the intended audience.

- **Intellectual Property:** Navigating the legal aspects of AI-generated content, such as copyright and ownership, is a crucial consideration for businesses.

- **Bias and Representation:** AI algorithms can perpetuate biases if not properly trained. It's important to ensure that the generated content is inclusive and represents diverse groups fairly.

The integration of AI in marketing, particularly in image and video generation, is still evolving. Advancements in AI technology promise even more sophisticated and efficient content creation capabilities. As AI tools become more accessible, they are likely to become a staple in the marketing toolkit, offering endless possibilities for creative and impactful marketing strategies.

Figure 3.5: Example of Video Generation using AI for marketing
Coca-Cola® Masterpiece seamlessly merges the realms of AI and art
(See Generate Video: Reading List)

3.5 AI and ChatGPT in Human Resources

Improving Recruitment and Hiring with AI:

AI has the potential to transform the recruitment and hiring process by streamlining and automating various tasks, such as resume screening, candidate matching, and interview scheduling. This can save HR professionals significant time and resources while ensuring that the most suitable candidates are considered for open positions.

By leveraging AI-powered algorithms, businesses can analyse large volumes of applicant data to identify patterns and trends, such as specific skills or experiences that correlate with successful hires. This enables companies to make more informed decisions and reduce the risk of hiring unsuitable candidates.

Enhancing Employee Engagement with ChatGPT:

Employee engagement is crucial for maintaining a productive and positive work environment. ChatGPT can be utilised to foster engagement by providing personalised training and development resources, facilitating communication between employees and management, and offering interactive onboarding experiences.

By generating human-like text, ChatGPT can create customised learning materials and provide real-time feedback to employees, ensuring that their professional development needs are met. Additionally, ChatGPT can facilitate communication channels between employees and management, enabling open and transparent discussions that help build trust and rapport.

AI for Performance Evaluation and Career:

Performance evaluation is a key aspect of HR management, and AI can play a significant role in streamlining and improving this process. AI-powered analytics can be used to track employee performance metrics, such as sales figures, project completion rates, or customer satisfaction scores, providing a more objective and data-driven approach to performance assessments.

Furthermore, AI can help identify skill gaps and areas of improvement for individual employees, enabling HR professionals to create targeted development plans that align with both company objectives and the employee's personal career goals. This personalised approach to career development can lead to increased job satisfaction, higher retention rates, and improved overall performance.

In conclusion, AI and ChatGPT offer numerous opportunities to enhance the effectiveness of human resources management. By improving recruitment and hiring processes, fostering employee engagement, and using AI for performance evaluation and career development, businesses can optimise their workforce and drive success. However, it is essential to consider the potential challenges associated with implementing these technologies, such as the need for extensive employee training, ethical considerations around data privacy, and the risk of overreliance on algorithms at the expense of human judgement.

Figure 3.6: 8 Ways of using ChatGPT for HR Teams
(Source: See Reading List)

3.6 AI and ChatGPT in Finance

Understanding the Role of AI in Finance:

AI has been increasingly integrated into the finance industry, driven by the need for improved efficiency, accuracy, and speed in decision-making processes. By automating various tasks, such as data entry, analysis, and forecasting, AI can significantly reduce human error and save time, allowing finance professionals to focus on more strategic tasks.

From algorithmic trading and portfolio management to customer service and financial planning, AI has the potential to transform the way businesses approach financial management, enabling them to make data-driven decisions and better navigate the complexities of the financial landscape.

ChatGPT for Financial Analysis and Reporting:

ChatGPT, as an advanced natural language processing tool, can greatly enhance financial analysis and reporting processes. By interpreting complex financial data and generating insightful, easy-to-understand reports, ChatGPT allows businesses to make informed decisions based on accurate and up-to-date information.

Additionally, ChatGPT can streamline the process of creating financial documents, such as earnings reports, budget plans, and investment proposals, saving time and resources while ensuring consistency and accuracy across all communications. This can be particularly beneficial for companies looking to communicate financial information to stakeholders and investors in a clear and effective manner.

AI for Fraud Detection and Risk Management:

Fraud detection and risk management are critical aspects of the finance industry, and AI can play a significant role in enhancing these processes. By analysing vast amounts of transactional data, AI-powered algorithms can identify unusual patterns or activities that may indicate fraudulent behaviour, enabling businesses to take proactive measures to prevent financial loss.

Similarly, AI can be used to assess and manage various financial risks, such as credit risk, market risk, and operational risk. By analysing historical data and identifying trends, AI can provide valuable insights into potential risk factors and suggest appropriate mitigation strategies. This enables businesses to make more informed decisions and minimise potential losses.

In conclusion, AI and ChatGPT offer numerous opportunities for businesses to enhance their financial management processes. By understanding the role of AI in finance, leveraging

ChatGPT for financial analysis and reporting, and implementing AI for fraud detection and risk management, businesses can improve efficiency, accuracy, and decision-making capabilities. However, it is important to consider the potential challenges associated with these technologies, such as data privacy concerns, the need for skilled personnel to manage and maintain AI systems, and the ethical implications of AI-driven decision-making.

AI Pricing Personalisation in Business and Banking:

AI is transforming the way businesses operate, and pricing is no exception. With the rise of AI-powered pricing personalization, businesses can now offer customised pricing strategies that cater to individual customers' needs and preferences. This not only improves customer satisfaction but can also increase revenue and profitability. In this section, we will explore the benefits of AI pricing personalisation and the ways businesses can implement it.

Improved Customer Satisfaction: By offering customised pricing strategies, businesses can provide a more personalised experience to their customers. Customers feel valued when they are offered pricing plans that match their specific needs and preferences. This leads to improved customer satisfaction, loyalty, and retention.

Increased Revenue: With AI pricing personalisation, businesses can optimise their pricing strategies to increase revenue. By analysing customer behaviour, businesses can identify pricing strategies that are more likely to lead to conversions. Additionally, personalised pricing can encourage customers to purchase more products or services, increasing overall revenue.

Improved Profitability: AI pricing personalisation can also help businesses improve their profitability. By optimising pricing strategies, businesses can reduce costs associated with under-priced products or services, overpriced products or services, or unsold inventory. This leads to improved profitability and better financial performance.

Ways to Implement AI Pricing Personalisation:

Collect Data: To implement AI pricing personalization, businesses must first collect relevant data on their customers' behaviour, preferences, and buying patterns. This includes data on past purchases, browsing behaviour, demographics, and other relevant information. Businesses can collect this data through various channels, including website analytics, social media, and customer surveys.

Analyse Data: Once data is collected, businesses must analyse it to identify patterns and insights that can inform pricing strategies. This involves using machine learning algorithms to process and analyse large volumes of data. Businesses can also use predictive modelling to anticipate customer behaviour and identify pricing strategies that are likely to lead to conversions.

Develop Customised Pricing Plans: Based on the insights gained from data analysis, businesses can develop customised pricing plans that cater to individual customers' needs and preferences. This can include offering discounts, promotions, and special offers based on customer behaviour and past purchases.

Test and Refine: As with any pricing strategy, it's important to test and refine AI-powered pricing personalization to ensure its effectiveness. This involves analysing the results of different pricing strategies and making adjustments as necessary.

AI pricing personalisation is the future of business. By offering customised pricing plans based on individual customer behaviour and preferences, businesses can improve customer satisfaction, increase revenue, and improve profitability. However, implementing AI pricing personalisation requires collecting and analysing large volumes of data, developing customised pricing plans, and testing and refining strategies. By following these steps, businesses can successfully implement AI pricing personalization and stay ahead of the competition.

AI-based Personalisation in Banking model:

AI-based personalisation in banking typically involves the use of machine learning algorithms to analyse large volumes of customer data and provide personalised recommendations or insights to customers. Here is a high-level model of the AI-based personalization process in banking:

Data Collection: The first step in the AI-based personalization process is collecting data on customers' financial behaviour. This data can include transaction history, account balances, spending patterns, and other relevant information.

Data Cleaning and Preparation: Once data is collected, it needs to be cleaned and prepared for analysis. This involves removing duplicates, correcting errors, and formatting data in a way that can be analysed by machine learning algorithms.

Data Analysis: After data is cleaned and prepared, machine learning algorithms can be used to analyse the data and identify patterns and insights. This involves using techniques such as clustering, regression, and classification to identify customer segments and preferences.

Personalisation: Based on the insights gained from data analysis, personalised recommendations or insights can be provided to customers. This can include offering customised financial products, providing personalised investment advice, or offering alerts or notifications based on customer behaviour.

Feedback Loop: As customers engage with personalised recommendations or insights, their behaviour and feedback can be used to refine the machine learning algorithms and improve the personalisation process over time. This feedback loop is essential to ensure that personalised recommendations continue to meet customers' evolving needs and preferences.

Overall, the AI-based personalisation model in banking involves collecting and analysing large volumes of data to provide personalised recommendations and insights to customers. By using machine learning algorithms to identify patterns and insights, banks can provide a more personalised experience to their customers and improve customer satisfaction and retention.

AI-based Personalisation in Banking:

Some case studies of AI-based personalisation in banking are:

JPMorgan Chase's Next Best Action Program: JPMorgan Chase launched the Next Best Action program, which uses machine learning algorithms to provide personalised recommendations to customers based on their financial behaviour. The program analyses customer data, such as spending patterns and account balances, to make recommendations on products and services that may be of interest to the customer. The program has helped the bank increase customer engagement and retention and has also resulted in higher cross-selling opportunities.

Wells Fargo's AI-powered Personalisation: Wells Fargo has been using AI to personalise customer experiences across various channels, including mobile apps and ATMs. For example, the bank uses machine learning algorithms to analyse customer data and offer personalised financial advice and alerts through its mobile app. The app can also personalise ATM experiences based on the customer's transaction history, such as offering cash denominations that are frequently used by the customer.

Bank of America's Erica Virtual Assistant: Bank of America has developed an AI-powered virtual assistant called Erica, which uses natural language processing to understand customer requests and provide personalised financial advice. Erica can help customers with a variety of tasks, such as checking account balances, paying bills, and transferring money. The virtual assistant also offers personalised insights based on the customer's spending habits, such as recommending ways to save money or pay off debt. Erica has been successful in improving customer engagement and satisfaction, with over 13 million users as of 2021.

These case studies demonstrate the potential benefits of AI-based personalisation in banking, such as increased customer engagement and retention, as well as improved cross-selling opportunities. However, they also highlight the importance of addressing challenges such as data quality and privacy concerns, bias and fairness issues, and customer acceptance and trust.

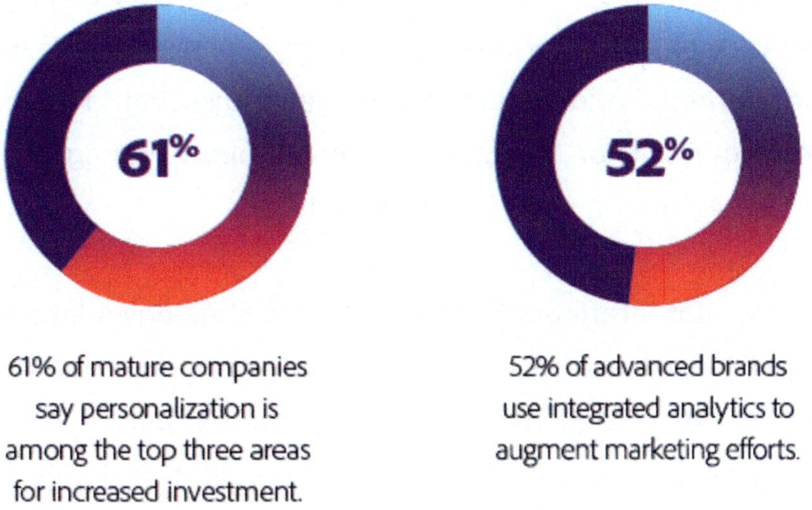

Figure 3.7: Importance of personalization and integration of analytics

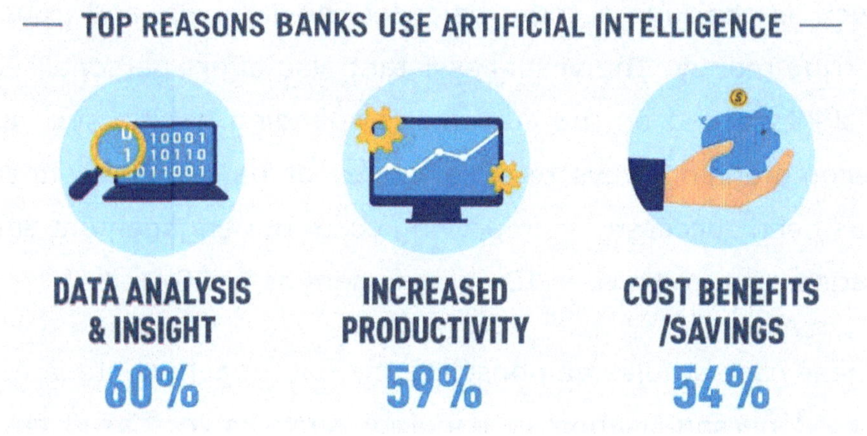

Figure 3.8: Top Reasons Banks use AI (Source: See Reading List)

3.7 Challenges of Implementing AI and ChatGPT in Businesses

Technical Challenges:

Implementing AI and ChatGPT in businesses comes with its own set of technical challenges. One of the primary concerns is the lack of skilled professionals with expertise in AI, machine learning, and natural language processing. This can make it difficult for businesses to implement, manage, and maintain AI-driven systems effectively.

Moreover, integrating AI and ChatGPT technologies into existing IT infrastructures can be a complex process, requiring extensive planning, resources, and compatibility testing. Businesses may also face challenges in scaling AI-driven solutions, particularly in the case of large organisations with extensive data and processing requirements.

Data Quality and Privacy Concerns:

Data quality and privacy are significant challenges when implementing AI and ChatGPT in businesses. In order to function effectively, AI-driven systems require access to large volumes of accurate, up-to-date data. However, businesses often face issues with data quality, including incomplete or inconsistent datasets, which can negatively impact the performance of AI algorithms.

Furthermore, data privacy concerns are increasingly prominent, particularly as AI-driven systems often process sensitive personal information. Businesses must ensure that they are compliant with data protection regulations, such as the General Data Protection Regulation (GDPR), and implement robust data security measures to protect user privacy.

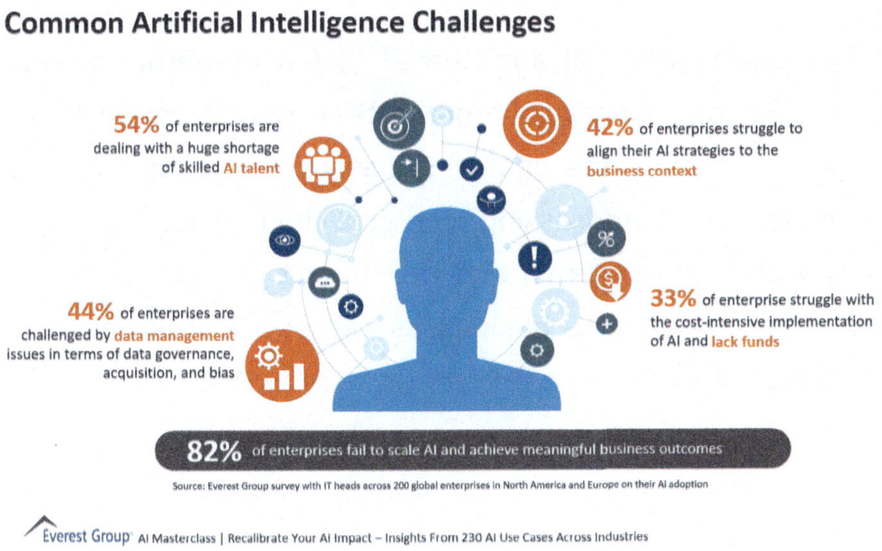

Figure 3.9: Common AI Challenges (Source: See Reading List)

Impact on Workforce and Organisational Culture

The adoption of AI and ChatGPT technologies can have a significant impact on a company's workforce and organisational culture. While these technologies have the potential to improve efficiency and streamline processes, they may also lead to job displacement and a reduction in human input in certain tasks.

To address these concerns, businesses must invest in re-skilling and upskilling initiatives for their workforce, ensuring that employees are equipped to work alongside AI-driven systems and adapt to new job roles. Additionally, organisations must foster a culture of continuous learning and innovation, encouraging employees to embrace new technologies and adapt to an evolving business landscape.

In conclusion, while AI and ChatGPT offer numerous opportunities for businesses to improve their operations, it is essential to consider the challenges associated with their implementation. By addressing technical challenges, data quality and privacy concerns, and the impact on workforce and organisational culture, businesses can successfully harness the power of AI and ChatGPT to drive growth and success.

Chapter 4:

AI and ChatGPT for SME, Start-up, and Innovation

4.1 AI for SME

There are several AI tools that can benefit small and medium-sized enterprises (SMEs) in different areas of their operations. Some commonly used AI tools for SMEs are as follows:

Customer Relationship Management (CRM) Systems: AI-powered CRM tools help SMEs manage customer data, track interactions, and automate various tasks. They can analyse customer behaviour, provide personalised recommendations, and automate marketing campaigns, leading to improved customer engagement and sales.

Chatbots and Virtual Assistants: AI-powered chatbots and virtual assistants can handle customer inquiries, provide support, and assist with basic tasks. They can be integrated into websites or messaging platforms to provide 24/7 customer service, reduce response times, and enhance the overall customer experience.

Natural Language Processing (NLP) Tools: NLP tools enable SMEs to process and understand human language. They can be used for sentiment analysis of customer feedback, text classification, language translation, and text summarization, helping SMEs gain valuable insights from textual data.

Data Analytics and Business Intelligence (BI) Tools: AI-powered data analytics and BI tools help SMEs extract meaningful insights from their data. They can analyse sales trends, customer behaviour, and market patterns, providing SMEs with actionable insights to make informed business decisions.

Predictive Analytics Tools: Predictive analytics tools use AI algorithms to analyse historical data and make predictions about future outcomes. SMEs can use these tools for demand forecasting, inventory management, and financial planning, optimising their operations and reducing costs.

Personalization and Recommendation Engines: AI-powered recommendation engines analyse customer preferences and behaviour to provide personalised product recommendations. SMEs can use these tools to offer tailored experiences, increase customer satisfaction, and drive sales.

Fraud Detection and Security Tools: AI-based fraud detection and security tools help SMEs identify suspicious activities, prevent fraud, and protect sensitive data. These tools use machine learning algorithms to detect anomalies and patterns that may indicate fraudulent behaviour.

It's important for SMEs to assess their specific needs and requirements before adopting AI tools. Integration, ease of use, and affordability should be considered when selecting the most suitable AI tools for their business operations.

4.2 ChatGPT for SME

ChatGPT can be a valuable tool for small and medium-sized enterprises (SMEs) in various ways. Here are some potential use cases:

Customer Support: SMEs can use ChatGPT to enhance their customer support services. The model can provide instant responses to customer inquiries, answer frequently asked questions, and assist with basic troubleshooting. This can help improve customer satisfaction, reduce response times, and free up human support agents to focus on more complex issues.

Sales and Marketing: ChatGPT can engage with potential customers, provide product information, and assist with sales inquiries. It can help guide customers through the sales process, offer personalised recommendations, and provide relevant information about products or services. This can enhance the overall customer experience and potentially increase sales conversion rates.

Information Retrieval: ChatGPT can act as a knowledge base for SMEs, providing information on products, services, company policies, and other relevant details. It can assist both customers and employees in finding the information they need quickly and accurately, reducing the need for manual searches or inquiries.

Appointment Scheduling: SMEs that rely on appointments, such as service-based businesses, can use ChatGPT to handle appointment scheduling. The model can check availability, book appointments, send reminders, and handle rescheduling requests. This can streamline the appointment booking process and improve efficiency.

Virtual Assistant: SMEs can employ ChatGPT as a virtual assistant to handle administrative tasks, such as managing calendars, setting reminders, sending notifications, and handling basic email communication. This can help optimise workflow, improve productivity, and reduce administrative overhead.

It's important to note that while ChatGPT can offer various benefits to SMEs, it may have limitations in handling complex or highly specific inquiries. SMEs should consider the specific needs of their business and carefully evaluate the implementation and integration of ChatGPT to ensure it aligns with their objectives and provides a positive user experience.

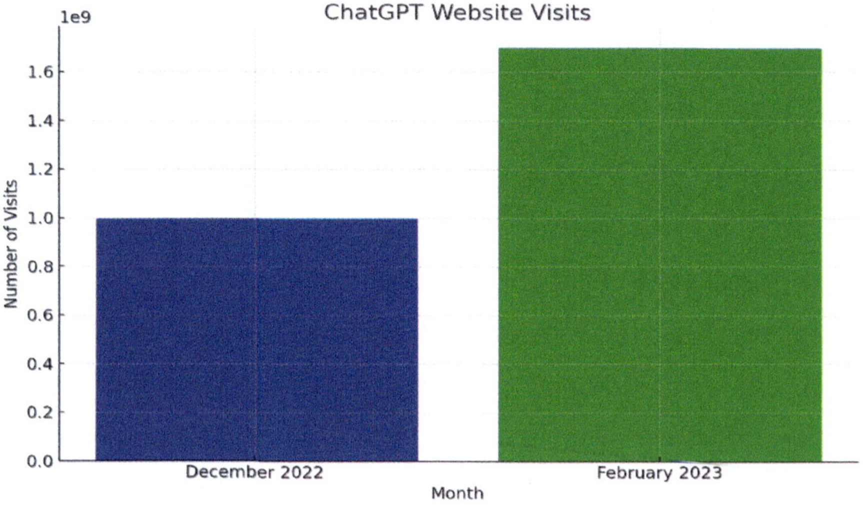

Figure 4.1: ChatGPT Website visit growth from Dec 2022-Feb 2023

Figure 4.2 presents a comprehensive overview of how AI and ChatGPT can be effectively utilized in Small and Medium-sized Enterprises (SMEs). The subsequent chapters delve into a range of business applications, illustrating how these technologies can be adapted and implemented in SME contexts.

This section provides detailed insights into various strategies and use cases, demonstrating the versatility and potential of AI and ChatGPT in enhancing SME operations.

Figure 4.2: AI and ChatGPT applications in SMEs

4.3 AI for Start-up and Innovation

AI can play a significant role in supporting start-ups and driving innovation. Here is some ways AI can benefit start-ups:

Product Development: AI can assist start-ups in developing innovative products by providing insights, automating tasks, and enabling new functionalities. It can help with tasks such as data analysis, market research, and identifying customer needs, which can lead to the creation of more relevant and competitive products.

Automation and Efficiency: AI technologies, such as robotic process automation (RPA), can automate repetitive and mundane tasks, freeing up valuable time for start-up teams to focus on strategic initiatives and creative problem-solving. This improves operational efficiency and allows start-ups to scale faster.

Personalisation and Customer Experience: AI-powered recommendation engines and chatbots can enhance customer experience by providing personalised product suggestions, answering inquiries promptly, and delivering tailored content. Start-ups can leverage AI to create personalised and engaging experiences, leading to increased customer satisfaction and loyalty.

Data Analysis and Insights: Start-ups often deal with large volumes of data. AI enables efficient data analysis, pattern recognition, and predictive modelling, allowing start-ups to gain valuable insights from their data. These insights can inform decision-making, identify trends, and uncover opportunities for innovation.

Cost Reduction: AI can help start-ups optimise their operations and reduce costs. By automating tasks, streamlining processes, and improving resource allocation, AI technologies can increase operational efficiency and decrease expenses.

Funding and Investor Attraction: AI-driven start-ups often attract attention from investors and venture capitalists due to the potential for disruptive innovation. Start-ups that leverage AI effectively can demonstrate their technological prowess and present compelling value propositions to investors, potentially securing funding for further growth and development.

Competitive Advantage: AI can provide start-ups with a competitive edge by enabling them to offer unique and differentiated products or services. By incorporating AI into their solutions, start-ups can differentiate themselves from competitors, attract customers, and establish themselves as innovative leaders in their industry.

It's worth noting that while AI offers numerous opportunities for start-ups, careful planning, consideration of ethical implications, and effective implementation strategies are essential to ensure successful integration and utilisation of AI technologies.

4.4 AI tools for Start-ups and Innovation

There are several AI tools that start-ups can leverage to drive innovation and enhance their operations. Here are some commonly used AI tools for start-ups:

Machine Learning Frameworks and Libraries: Open-source machine learning frameworks like TensorFlow and PyTorch provide start-ups with the building blocks for developing and deploying AI models. These tools offer a wide range of algorithms and resources for tasks such as image recognition, natural language processing, and predictive modelling.

Cloud AI Services: Cloud-based AI services, such as Amazon Web Services (AWS) AI, Google Cloud AI, and Microsoft Azure AI, offer start-ups access to pre-trained AI models, scalable infrastructure, and APIs for integrating AI capabilities into their applications. These services provide cost-effective and easily accessible AI tools without requiring extensive infrastructure investment.

Natural Language Processing (NLP) Tools: NLP tools like spaCy, NLTK, and Stanford NLP allow start-ups to process and analyse text data, extract insights, perform sentiment analysis, and build language models. These tools are particularly useful for start-ups focused on content analysis, customer feedback analysis, chatbots, or language-based applications.

Computer Vision Tools: Computer vision frameworks like OpenCV, Microsoft Azure Computer Vision, and Google Cloud Vision enable start-ups to analyse and understand visual content. These tools can be used for tasks such as object detection, image recognition, facial recognition, and video analysis.

Chatbot Development Platforms: Chatbot development platforms like Dialogflow, Microsoft Bot Framework, and IBM Watson Assistant help start-ups build and deploy conversational AI agents. These tools enable start-ups to create chatbots that can handle customer inquiries, provide support, and automate interactions, enhancing customer engagement and service delivery.

Data Analytics and Visualisation Tools: Data analytics and visualisation platforms like Tableau, Power BI, and Google Data Studio allow start-ups to analyse and visualise their data. These tools help identify patterns, derive insights, and communicate data-driven findings effectively, supporting data-driven decision-making and innovation.

Automated Machine Learning (AutoML) Platforms:

AutoML platforms like H2O.ai and Data Robot simplify the process of building AI models by automating tasks such as feature engineering, model selection, and hyperparameter tuning. Start-ups with limited resources can leverage these tools to accelerate model development and deployment.

It's important for start-ups to consider their specific needs, available resources, and the scalability of AI tools when selecting the most appropriate ones for their innovation goals. It's also advisable to stay up-to-date with the latest AI advancements and research to take advantage of emerging tools and techniques.

4.5 ChatGPT for Start-ups and Innovation

ChatGPT can indeed be a valuable tool for fostering innovation within start-ups and organisations. Here are some ways ChatGPT can support innovation:

Ideation and Brainstorming: ChatGPT can be used as a virtual brainstorming partner, helping to generate ideas, explore different perspectives, and stimulate creativity. By providing prompts or questions, ChatGPT can assist in generating innovative solutions or approaches to various challenges.

Prototyping and Concept Validation: Start-ups can use ChatGPT to prototype and validate new concepts or features. By simulating conversations or interactions with potential users, ChatGPT can gather feedback, refine ideas, and identify potential issues early in the development process.

User Experience Design: ChatGPT can aid in designing user experiences by simulating conversations with potential users. Start-ups can test different user interfaces, gather feedback on the ease of use, and identify areas for improvement. This iterative feedback loop can enhance the overall user experience and drive innovation in product design.

Market Research and Customer Insights: ChatGPT can engage in conversations with users or potential customers to gather valuable insights. Start-ups can use ChatGPT to conduct surveys, simulate user interviews, or collect feedback on product features, preferences, and pain points. This helps in understanding customer needs and preferences, which can inform innovation strategies.

Rapid Prototyping and MVP Development: ChatGPT can assist in the rapid prototyping and development of minimum viable products (MVPs). Start-ups can leverage ChatGPT's conversational capabilities to quickly create interactive prototypes or proof-of-concept demos, allowing for iterative testing and validation of new product ideas.

Product Personalisation and Recommendation:

ChatGPT can help deliver personalised recommendations or tailored experiences to users. By understanding user preferences and behaviour, ChatGPT can provide relevant suggestions, content, or product recommendations, fostering innovation in personalised user interactions.

Continuous Learning and Improvement: ChatGPT can be fine-tuned and continuously improved based on user feedback and real-world usage. By gathering data on user interactions, start-ups can train ChatGPT to become more contextually aware, provide better responses, and adapt to evolving user needs, fostering innovation in the AI-powered conversational experience.

It's important to note that while ChatGPT can be a powerful tool for innovation, it may have limitations in handling complex or highly specific tasks. Startups should consider the specific use cases, data privacy, and ethical considerations when utilising ChatGPT for innovation purposes.

Chapter 5:

Prompt Engineering in Business Growth

5.1 Understanding Prompt Engineering

Prompt engineering is the skilful crafting of input data or queries to elicit desired outputs from AI models. In business, this means using specific, targeted prompts to generate useful information, creative content, or problem-solving ideas from AI systems.

Basics of Prompt Engineering: Prompt engineering is more than just asking questions. It involves understanding the capabilities and limitations of AI models, and how the framing of a prompt can significantly alter the results.

Fundamental Principles of Effective Prompt Crafting

Clarity and Specificity: The most effective prompts are clear and specific. They precisely define what is expected from the AI model, leaving little room for misinterpretation. This means using precise language and being explicit about the desired outcome.

Understanding Model Capabilities and Limitations: A key principle is understanding the capabilities and limitations of the AI model being used. This involves knowing what the model can and cannot do, and crafting prompts that play to its strengths while avoiding its weaknesses.

Context and Relevance: Effective prompts provide enough context to guide the AI towards the desired output. This might include background information, specific scenarios, or detailed descriptions, ensuring the response is relevant and focused.

Creativity and Innovation: While prompts should be clear and specific, they also need to leave room for creativity and innovation, especially in tasks requiring novel or out-of-the-box thinking. This balance can be achieved by posing open-ended questions that encourage creative responses.

Iterative Refinement: Prompt crafting is often an iterative process. Based on the initial output, prompts may need to be adjusted and refined. This principle involves evaluating the effectiveness of a prompt and tweaking it as needed to improve the results.

Ethical Considerations: It's essential to consider the ethical implications of prompts, especially those that might lead to biased or harmful outputs. Prompts should be crafted to promote fairness, accuracy, and respect for privacy and ethical norms.

Goal Alignment: Prompts must align with the overarching goals of the task at hand. This means understanding the end objective and crafting prompts that steer the AI towards outputs that support these goals.

Balancing Brevity with Detail: An effective prompt strikes a balance between being concise and providing necessary detail. Overly long prompts can be confusing, while too brief prompts may not provide enough guidance, leading to irrelevant or off-target outputs.

Anticipating User Intent: In crafting prompts, it's crucial to anticipate the user's intent or need. This involves thinking about the user's perspective and what they are likely to expect or need from the AI's response.

Scalability and Flexibility: Finally, good prompts are scalable and flexible. They should work well across different contexts or datasets and be adaptable to changing requirements or conditions.

These principles form the foundation of effective prompt crafting, enabling the creation of inputs that lead to accurate, relevant, and insightful outputs from AI models.

5.2 Applications in Marketing and Advertising

In the field of marketing, prompt engineering has revolutionized content creation and customer engagement strategies.

Generating Customized Content:

"Generating Customized Content" refers to the use of AI in creating personalized advertising content, a technique that has become increasingly established in the business world. This process involves leveraging AI's advanced algorithms to tailor marketing messages and materials to specific segments of the audience, or even individual consumers, based on various factors. Detailed explanation of these are given below:

Data Analysis and Consumer Insights:

- AI systems analyse vast amounts of data, including consumer behaviour, purchase history, browsing patterns, and social media interactions.
- This analysis helps in understanding individual preferences, interests, and behaviours.

Segmentation and Targeting:

- Based on the insights gathered, AI categorizes consumers into different segments.
- These segments could be based on demographics, psychographics, behavioural patterns, or a combination of these factors.

Personalization of Content:

- AI then generates content that is specifically tailored to the interests and preferences of each segment or individual.

- This could include personalized email marketing messages, targeted social media ads, customized product recommendations, or even dynamic website content.

Dynamic Content Creation:

- AI can dynamically alter content in real-time based on user interaction. For example, if a user spends time looking at a specific product, the AI might display ads or send emails related to that product.
- The content could vary in terms of visuals, text, offers, and even the tone and style of communication to better resonate with the targeted audience.

A/B Testing and Optimization:

- AI tools can conduct A/B testing on various content versions to determine which performs better for different audience segments.
- Based on the results, AI continuously optimizes the content strategy for better engagement and conversion rates.

Integration Across Channels:

- Personalized content is not limited to one platform; AI ensures a cohesive and personalized experience across all channels, whether it's email, social media, websites, or mobile apps.
- This creates a consistent and seamless customer journey.

Predictive Analysis for Future Campaigns:

- AI can predict future consumer behaviours and preferences based on historical data, helping businesses stay ahead in their content strategy.
- This predictive capability allows for proactive content creation, anticipating customer needs even before they arise.

Ethical and Privacy Considerations:

- While leveraging data for personalization, businesses must navigate the fine line of privacy and consent.
- AI systems are designed to comply with data protection laws and ethical standards, ensuring that personalization does not breach consumer privacy.

In essence, the process of generating customized content using AI represents a shift from a one-size-fits-all approach to a more targeted, individualized marketing strategy. This not only enhances the relevance and effectiveness of advertising campaigns but also fosters a deeper connection between the brand and its customers.

Enhancing Customer Interaction:

Prompt engineering has enabled more dynamic and responsive customer service. In the realm of customer service, the application of well-crafted prompts in AI systems has been transformative, significantly improving the customer experience in several keyways:

Understanding Customer Needs Quickly: AI systems equipped with advanced natural language processing capabilities can quickly interpret and understand customer queries. When powered by carefully designed prompts, these AI systems can discern the context and specifics of customer requests, leading to more accurate and relevant responses.

Personalized Responses: Well-crafted prompts enable AI to tailor responses based on the customer's history, preferences, or specific circumstances. This personalization makes interactions feel more engaging and human-like, enhancing customer satisfaction.

Efficiency in Handling Queries: AI systems, prompted correctly, can handle a large volume of queries simultaneously, providing instant responses. This efficiency is crucial in reducing wait times and improving the overall customer experience, especially during peak hours or for common inquiries that don't require human intervention.

Consistency in Service Quality: Unlike human customer service representatives who might have varying levels of expertise or might be influenced by emotions or fatigue, AI systems maintain a consistent quality of responses. Well-crafted prompts ensure that this consistency is aligned with the company's standards and customer service policies.

Availability and Accessibility: AI-driven customer service is available 24/7, providing customers with the flexibility to seek help at their convenience. This round-the-clock availability, supported by effective prompt engineering, significantly improves accessibility and convenience for customers.

Scalability for Diverse Queries: Good prompts are designed to equip AI systems with the ability to scale and adapt to a wide range of queries, from simple FAQ-type questions to more complex, situation-specific issues. This scalability ensures that customers receive relevant help regardless of the complexity of their needs.

Continuous Learning and Improvement: AI systems can learn from interactions and improve over time. With each query, the AI refines its understanding and response accuracy, ensuring that the customer service experience keeps getting better, a process further enhanced by ongoing refinement of the prompts.

Integration with Omnichannel Support: Prompt engineering in AI can be tailored to integrate seamlessly with various channels of customer support, such as email, chat, social media, or phone, providing a unified and cohesive customer experience.

By harnessing well-crafted prompts, AI in customer service not only addresses the immediate needs of customers but also plays a pivotal role in building a sustainable, efficient, and highly responsive customer service ecosystem. This leads to a notable improvement in customer satisfaction, loyalty, and overall experience with the brand.

5.3 Enhancing Product Development

The role of prompt engineering in product development extends beyond just improving communication. It serves as a pivotal tool for fostering innovation and creativity in the creation and enhancement of products. Here's a more detailed explanation:

Ideation and Conceptualization:

- **Prompt-Driven Brainstorming:** AI, guided by specific prompts, can assist in brainstorming sessions by generating a wide range of ideas and concepts. These prompts could ask the AI to consider current market trends, consumer needs, or technological possibilities, leading to innovative product ideas.
- **Combining Diverse Elements:** Through prompts, AI can combine elements from different domains or industries to create novel product concepts. For example, a prompt might ask the AI to integrate features from the gaming industry into fitness equipment.

Design and Prototyping:

- **Rapid Prototype Generation:** AI can use prompts to quickly generate models or prototypes based on specified criteria, such as material, cost, functionality, or aesthetic appeal. This significantly speeds up the design process.

- **Simulation and Testing:** Prompts can direct AI to simulate how a product might perform under various conditions, providing valuable insights during the design phase and reducing the need for physical prototypes.

Customization and Personalization:

- **Tailoring Products to Customer Preferences:** AI can analyse consumer data and generate prompts that lead to the development of customized or personalized products, catering to specific consumer preferences or needs.

- **Adaptive Design Solutions:** AI can use prompts to create adaptive designs, which can evolve based on user feedback or changing market demands.

Efficiency and Cost Reduction:

- **Streamlining the Development Process:** Prompt engineering can help identify the most efficient and cost-effective methods for product development, from material selection to manufacturing processes.

- **Waste Reduction:** AI can suggest design alterations or material choices that minimize waste, aligning with sustainability goals.

Market Analysis and Fit:

- **Predictive Market Analysis:** AI can be prompted to analyse market trends and predict future demands, helping in designing products that are more likely to succeed in the market.
- **Competitor Analysis:** AI can evaluate competitors' products and identify gaps or opportunities for innovation in the market.

Collaboration and Cross-Disciplinary Insights:

- **Enhancing Team Collaboration:** By providing diverse insights and perspectives, AI can enhance collaboration among design teams, engineers, and marketers.
- **Cross-Disciplinary Learning:** AI, through prompts, can incorporate knowledge from various fields (like environmental science, ergonomics, or sociology) into the product development process.

In summary, prompt engineering in product development is about leveraging AI to not only generate innovative ideas and designs but also to streamline the development process, create products that are more in tune with market needs, and ensure these products are developed efficiently and sustainably. This approach represents a significant shift in how products are conceived, designed, and brought to market, offering a competitive edge in today's rapidly evolving business landscape.

5.4 Strategic Decision Making

The incorporation of AI in decision-making processes, guided by prompt engineering, has revolutionized how businesses approach strategic planning and problem-solving. This transformation can be understood in greater detail through several key aspects:

Data Analysis and Insight Generation:

- **Comprehensive Data Interpretation:** AI systems, prompted appropriately, can analyse vast amounts of data – from market trends to customer feedback – and extract actionable insights. This process involves not just aggregating data but also interpreting it in ways that are meaningful for business decisions.

- **Real-time Analytics:** Prompt engineering enables AI to provide real-time analytics, crucial for making timely decisions in a fast-paced business environment.

Predictive Modelling and Forecasting:

- **Future Trends Prediction:** AI can use historical data to predict future market trends, consumer behaviours, or potential risks. Prompts can guide the AI to focus on specific areas of interest or concern for the business.

- **Scenario Analysis:** AI can simulate various scenarios based on different variables and inputs. For instance, a prompt could ask the AI to analyse how changes in market conditions might affect sales or revenue.

Risk Assessment and Management:

- **Identifying Potential Risks:** AI can be prompted to scan the business and market environment to identify potential risks, including financial, operational, or reputational risks.
- **Mitigation Strategy Development:** Beyond identification, AI can suggest strategies to mitigate these risks, helping businesses to prepare for and manage potential challenges effectively.

Decision Support and Optimization:

- **Optimizing Business Processes:** AI can assist in identifying areas within business processes that can be optimized for efficiency, cost savings, or better performance.

- **Supporting Complex Decisions:** For complex decision-making, AI can evaluate multiple variables and outcomes, providing businesses with a comprehensive view to make informed decisions.

Enhancing Creativity in Strategic Planning:

- **Creative Problem Solving:** Prompt engineering can stimulate AI to think outside traditional frameworks, offering creative solutions to business challenges.

- **Innovative Strategy Development:** AI can propose innovative strategies that might not be immediately apparent to human analysts, potentially opening new avenues for business growth.

Ethical and Responsible Decision-Making:

- **Ethical Considerations:** AI systems can be prompted to consider ethical implications in decision-making processes, ensuring that strategies align with the company's ethical standards and social responsibilities.

- **Bias Mitigation:** Prompt engineering can help in identifying and mitigating biases in decision-making, leading to more fair and objective business decisions.

Collaborative Decision-Making:

- **Enhancing Team Collaboration:** AI can provide insights that enhance collaboration among different departments, ensuring that decisions are well-informed and balanced.

- **Integrating Diverse Perspectives:** AI, through comprehensive data analysis, can integrate perspectives from various stakeholders, leading to more holistic and inclusive decision-making.

In summary, strategic decision-making through prompt engineering in AI represents a shift towards more data-driven, efficient, and innovative business processes. It empowers businesses to make more informed, strategic, and forward-looking decisions, significantly enhancing their ability to adapt and thrive in an increasingly complex and competitive business environment.

5.5 Future Prospects and Challenges of Prompt Engineering in Business

As we look towards the future of prompt engineering in business, it's essential to consider both the emerging opportunities and the challenges that lie ahead. This evolving field presents a landscape filled with potential for growth and innovation, alongside significant hurdles that need to be addressed.

Future Prospects:

Advanced AI Capabilities

- **Evolution of AI Models:** We can expect AI models to become more sophisticated, understanding and responding to prompts with greater accuracy and nuance.

- **Integration of AI in More Business Areas:** AI's reach will likely extend into more aspects of business operations, offering new ways to optimize processes and decision-making.

Customization and Personalization

- **Hyper-Personalization:** The ability to create highly personalized customer experiences through prompt engineering will continue to grow, leading to more effective marketing and customer engagement.
- **Individualized Products and Services:** We will see an increase in the use of AI to design products and services tailored to individual preferences and needs.

Real-Time Decision Making and Responsiveness

- **Faster Business Responses:** With improvements in AI, businesses will be able to respond to market changes and customer needs more quickly.
- **Predictive and Proactive Strategies:** AI will increasingly be able to predict trends and challenges, allowing businesses to be proactive rather than reactive.

Expansion into New Markets and Industries

- **Broader Application:** The use of prompt engineering will spread to industries that have been slower to adopt AI, offering new opportunities for growth and innovation.

Improvements in Ethical AI and Bias Mitigation

- **Ethical AI Development:** There will be a greater focus on developing AI that is ethical and unbiased, with prompt engineering playing a crucial role in shaping these efforts.

Challenges:

Data Privacy and Security

- **Handling Sensitive Information:** As AI systems process more personal data, ensuring privacy and security will become increasingly challenging.
- **Regulatory Compliance:** Adhering to evolving data protection laws and regulations will be a key concern for businesses using AI.

Complexity in AI Management

- **Managing Advanced AI Systems:** As AI becomes more complex, the challenge of managing and maintaining these systems effectively will grow.
- **Skill Gap:** There will be a growing need for skilled professionals who can effectively work with advanced AI systems, potentially leading to a skills gap.

Ethical and Societal Implications

- **Addressing Bias:** Despite advancements, eliminating bias in AI will remain a challenge.

- **Ethical Use of AI:** Ensuring that AI is used ethically, especially in sensitive areas like employment, healthcare, and law enforcement, will be a continuous challenge.

Technological Limitations and Reliability

- **Reliability of AI Responses:** Ensuring that AI responses are reliable and accurate, especially in critical decision-making scenarios, will be crucial.
- **Limitations in Understanding Context:** AI may still struggle with understanding complex human contexts, nuances, and emotions.

Economic and Social Impact

- **Impact on Employment:** The increasing use of AI in businesses could have significant implications for employment and workforce dynamics.
- **Digital Divide:** The gap between AI-advanced businesses and those lagging in AI adoption could widen, leading to a digital divide.

In conclusion, the future of prompt engineering in business is poised for significant growth and transformation, offering exciting opportunities for innovation and efficiency. However, navigating the accompanying challenges, especially in ethical, technical, and societal aspects, will be crucial for realizing its full potential.

5.6 Case Studies: Prompt Engineering in Action

In this section, we delve into real-world examples that illustrate how businesses have successfully implemented prompt engineering to drive innovation, improve operations, and achieve notable results. These case studies provide insights into the practical application of prompt engineering in various industries and contexts.

Case Study 1: E-Commerce Giant - Enhanced Product Recommendation System

- **Background:** A leading e-commerce company sought to improve its product recommendation engine.
- **Prompt Used:** "Generate personalized product recommendations based on individual customer behaviours, purchase history, and browsing patterns, with a focus on increasing repeat purchase rates."
- **Possible Outcome:** The AI system, utilizing this prompt, significantly enhanced the relevance of product suggestions, leading to a 35% increase in customer repeat purchase rates. The benefit of this specific prompt was its focus on individualized customer data, leading to more accurate recommendations compared to generic algorithms.

Case Study 2: Global Bank - Advanced Credit Risk Analysis

- **Background:** A multinational bank wanted to refine its credit risk assessment process for loan applications.
- **Prompt Used:** "Evaluate credit risk by integrating applicants' financial history, current credit scores, and economic trends, aiming to minimize default risk while expanding customer base."
- **Possible Outcome:** The AI-enhanced risk assessment resulted in a 20% reduction in loan defaults and a 15% growth in approved loans. This prompt's comprehensive approach to risk assessment proved more effective than traditional, less nuanced methods, leading to better risk management and business expansion.

Case Study 3: Health Tech Company - Improved Disease Detection

- **Background:** A health technology company focused on enhancing early disease detection accuracy in medical imaging.
- **Prompt Used:** "Identify early signs of specific diseases in medical images, considering patient medical history and current clinical research, to assist radiologists in early diagnosis."

- **Possible Outcome:** The AI tool achieved a 40% improvement in early disease detection accuracy. This prompt's emphasis on combining imaging with patient history and research led to higher diagnostic accuracy compared to traditional image-only analysis.

Case Study 4: Online Retailer - Optimized Customer Service

- **Background:** An online retail giant needed to upgrade its customer service response system.
- **Prompt Used:** "Deliver accurate and empathetic responses to customer inquiries, focusing on reducing response time and enhancing customer satisfaction."
- **Possible Outcome:** The AI-driven system decreased response times by 60% and improved customer satisfaction scores by 25%. This prompt's dual focus on accuracy and empathy offered a more balanced approach than standard automated responses, aligning better with customer expectations.

Case Study 5: Industrial Manufacturer - Streamlined Production Processes

- **Background:** An industrial manufacturer aimed to streamline its production line for efficiency and reduced waste.

- **Prompt Used:** "Analyse real-time production data to identify inefficiencies and recommend actionable improvements, targeting a reduction in waste and cost while maximizing output."
- **Possible Outcome:** The AI recommendations led to a 25% increase in production efficiency and a 30% reduction in waste. This prompt's real-time data analysis provided a more dynamic and effective approach to process optimization compared to traditional periodic reviews.

Case Study 6: Digital Marketing Firm - Targeted Campaign Analysis

- **Background:** A digital marketing firm sought to enhance the effectiveness of its advertising campaigns.
- **Prompt Used:** "Conduct a multi-dimensional analysis of campaign data across various channels, focusing on consumer engagement and conversion efficiency, to refine marketing strategies."
- **Possible Outcome:** The AI-enabled analysis resulted in a 30% improvement in campaign conversion rates. The prompt's comprehensive and multi-dimensional approach to data analysis offered deeper insights than conventional single-factor analyses, leading to more effective marketing strategies.

In each case study, the specific prompt used played a critical role in determining the outcome. These prompts were designed not only to guide AI in performing complex tasks but also to focus on aspects that were crucial for each business's needs. These case studies showcase the diverse applications of prompt engineering across different sectors, demonstrating its capability to enhance customer experiences, improve operational efficiency, and drive data-driven decision-making.

The advantages of using these well-crafted prompts over traditional methods lie in their ability to provide more accurate, personalized, and efficient solutions, ultimately leading to better business results and customer experiences.

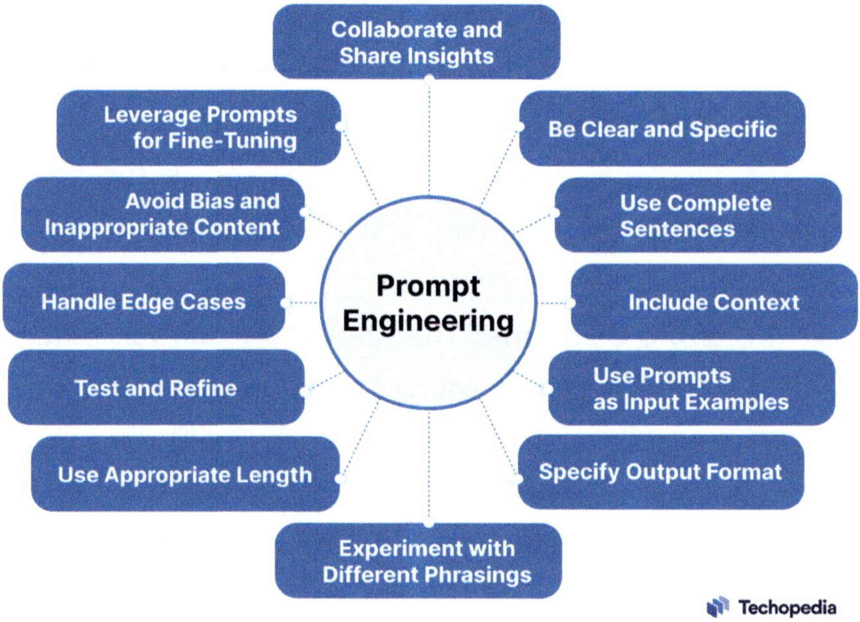

Figure 5.1: Prompt Engineering Best Practices
(Source: See Reading List)

Chapter 6:

Ethics, Trends and Recommendations

6.1 AI and ChatGPT Governance and Ethics

Ethical Considerations in AI and ChatGPT:

As AI and ChatGPT become more integrated into various aspects of business operations, it is crucial to address the ethical considerations associated with their deployment. Some of the primary concerns to deploy responsible AI systems include:

Bias and fairness: AI models may unintentionally propagate existing biases and stereotypes present in the training data, leading to unfair treatment or discrimination. Businesses must adopt strategies to minimise and mitigate biases in AI systems.

Transparency and explainability: Understanding the decision-making process of AI models is essential to ensure accountability and trust. Companies should prioritise transparency and explainability in their AI systems to prevent "black box" issues.

Data privacy and security: Ensuring the protection of user data and maintaining privacy is of paramount importance. Businesses must implement robust data security measures and adhere to relevant data protection regulations.

Implementing Responsible AI Practices in Business:

To address the ethical challenges associated with AI and ChatGPT, businesses should adopt responsible AI practices, such as:

Developing a clear AI strategy: Companies should establish a comprehensive AI strategy that outlines their objectives, ethical principles, and guidelines for deploying responsible AI systems.

Integrating ethics into AI design: Ethical considerations should be an integral part of the AI development process, from data collection to model training and deployment.

Establishing AI governance structures: Implementing robust governance structures can help businesses oversee AI projects, assess potential risks, and ensure compliance with ethical standards and regulations.

Investing in employee training and education: Providing employees with the necessary knowledge and skills to work with AI responsibly will help businesses navigate the ethical challenges associated with AI deployment.

Navigating Legal and Regulatory Frameworks for AI

As AI technologies continue to advance, businesses must navigate the evolving legal and regulatory landscape surrounding AI:

Compliance with data protection laws: Companies should be aware of the data protection regulations in the jurisdictions they operate, such as the General Data Protection Regulation (GDPR) in the European Union or the California Consumer Privacy Act (CCPA) in the United States.

Legal Compliance: The integration of AI in business operations has necessitated a re-evaluation of legal compliance frameworks. As AI technologies evolve, they bring forth unique challenges in terms of privacy, data protection, and ethical considerations. Two significant regulatory frameworks that businesses must consider are the European Union's AI Act and the standards set by the National Institute of Standards and Technology (NIST) in the UK and USA.

Intellectual property rights: AI-generated content and inventions may raise complex questions about intellectual property rights. Businesses should stay informed about the legal implications of AI-generated works and protect their interests accordingly.

Liability for AI decisions: Determining liability for decisions made by AI systems can be challenging. Companies must be prepared to address potential disputes and litigation arising from AI-related decisions.

By adopting responsible AI practices, addressing ethical considerations, and navigating the legal and regulatory frameworks, businesses can harness the potential of AI and ChatGPT while mitigating risks and ensuring long-term success.

6.2 Future of AI and ChatGPT in Businesses

Trends and Innovations in AI and ChatGPT

As AI and ChatGPT continue to evolve, several trends and innovations are shaping the future of these technologies in businesses:

- **Advanced natural language processing (NLP)**: Ongoing advancements in NLP will allow AI systems like ChatGPT to better understand and respond to human language, resulting in more natural and effective interactions.

- **Emotional intelligence and sentiment analysis**: Future AI systems will likely incorporate emotional intelligence to better gauge users' emotions and tailor responses accordingly. This will lead to more personalised and empathetic customer interactions.

- **Improved explainability**: As businesses become more reliant on AI, there will be a growing demand for explainable AI systems that provide insight into their decision-making processes, enabling greater transparency and accountability.
- **Integration with other emerging technologies**: AI and ChatGPT will likely be integrated with other cutting-edge technologies such as blockchain, Internet of Things (IoT), and quantum computing, further enhancing their capabilities and applications.

Future of AI and ChatGPT in Business

Based on the ongoing trends and innovations in AI and ChatGPT, we can make several predictions about their future in businesses:

- **Increased AI adoption across industrie**s: As AI and ChatGPT become more advanced and accessible, businesses across various sectors will increasingly adopt these technologies to optimise operations, enhance decision-making, and improve customer experiences.
- **Greater collaboration between humans and AI**: The future of work will likely involve more collaboration between humans and AI systems, with each party focusing on tasks they excel at. AI will augment human capabilities rather than replace them entirely.

- **Ethical and regulatory developments**: As AI and ChatGPT become more prevalent in businesses, there will likely be increased focus on developing ethical guidelines and regulatory frameworks to ensure responsible AI deployment and address potential concerns.
- **Customisation and personalisation**: AI and ChatGPT will enable businesses to deliver highly customised products and services, providing customers with more personalised experiences that cater to their unique preferences and needs.
- **New business models and opportunities**: The widespread adoption of AI and ChatGPT will create new business models and opportunities, with companies leveraging these technologies to innovate and disrupt traditional industries.

6.3 Recommendations

Throughout this book, we have presented the numerous opportunities and challenges associated with the adoption of AI and ChatGPT in the business landscape. Some of the key takeaways include:

- AI and ChatGPT have the potential to revolutionise various industries, such as healthcare, education, manufacturing, and FinTech, by improving efficiency, personalisation, and decision-making.

- The implementation of AI and ChatGPT in business can lead to significant benefits, including cost reduction, enhanced customer experience, and streamlined operations.
- The ethical considerations associated with AI and ChatGPT, such as bias and fairness, transparency, and data privacy, must be addressed to ensure responsible AI deployment.
- Navigating the evolving legal and regulatory landscape is essential for businesses looking to implement AI and ChatGPT, as they must comply with data protection laws, intellectual property rights, and liability concerns.

Final Thoughts and Recommendations:

As AI and ChatGPT continue to advance, businesses that strategically adopt these technologies will likely gain a competitive edge in their respective industries. To successfully implement AI and ChatGPT, we recommend the following steps:

- **Develop a clear AI strategy**: Outline your objectives, ethical principles, and guidelines for AI deployment. This strategy will provide a roadmap for integrating AI and ChatGPT into your business operations.
- **Invest in talent and employee education**: Building a team with the necessary knowledge and skills to work with AI responsibly is crucial. Provide training and education to ensure your workforce can navigate the challenges associated with AI deployment.

- **Adopt responsible AI practices**: Integrate ethical considerations into the AI development process and establish robust governance structures to oversee AI projects and assess potential risks.
- **Stay informed about legal and regulatory frameworks**: Monitor the evolving legal landscape surrounding AI and ensure compliance with data protection regulations, intellectual property rights, and liability concerns.
- **Collaborate and learn from others**: Engage with industry peers, join AI-focused forums, and attend conferences to share knowledge, learn from best practices, and stay up to date with the latest advancements in AI and ChatGPT.

By following these recommendations and addressing the challenges outlined in this book, businesses can harness the transformative potential of AI and ChatGPT while minimising risks and fostering long-term success.

Recommended Reading List & Source Links

- "Artificial Intelligence: A Guide for Thinking Humans" by Melanie Mitchell - An accessible book offering a critical look at AI's capabilities and limitations.
- "Predictive Analytics: The Power to Predict Who Will Click, Buy, Lie, or Die" by Eric Siegel - Insightful exploration of predictive analytics in business.
- "Life 3.0: Being Human in the Age of Artificial Intelligence" by Max Tegmark - Discusses AI's impact on the future of life on Earth and beyond.
- "The Master Algorithm: How the Quest for the Ultimate Learning Machine Will Remake Our World" by Pedro Domingos - A comprehensive guide to machine learning.
- "Superintelligence: Paths, Dangers, Strategies" by Nick Bostrom - Examines the future of AI and its potential impact on humanity.
- Harvard Business Review articles on AI and Machine Learning - Provides practical insights and case studies on AI in business contexts.
- McKinsey Global Institute Report: "Artificial Intelligence: The Next Digital Frontier?" - Offers a deep dive into AI's impact on industries and economies.
- "AI Superpowers: China, Silicon Valley, and the New World Order" by Kai-Fu Lee - Explores the AI race between China and the US.
- "Human + Machine: Reimagining Work in the Age of AI" by Paul R. Daugherty and H. James Wilson - Focuses on the collaboration between humans and AI in the workplace.

- Figure 1.2:

https://nextnature.net/story/2013/what-ant-colony-networks-can-tell-us-about-what%E2%80%99s-next-for-digital-networks

- Figure 3.2:

https://www.milliman.com/en/insight/explainable-ai-in-fraud-detection

- Figure 3.3:

https://zapier.com/blog/ai-marketing/

- Figure 3.5:

https://www.youtube.com/watch?v=VGa1imApfdg

- Figure 3.6:

https://www.frankli.io/post/ai-in-hr-chatgpt-prompts-hr-operations

- Figure 3.8:

https://www.paymentscardsandmobile.com/how-is-ai-changing-the-banking-in-dustry/

- Figure 3.9:

https://www.everestgrp.com/2019-12-common-artificial-intelligence-challenges-market-insights-52133.html

- Figure 5.1:

https://www.techopedia.com/definition/prompt-engineering

End

Printed in Great Britain
by Amazon

36671190R00079